3-5 1-

world poverty and development: a survey of american opinion

Paul A. Laudicina
with a Foreword
by John W. Sewell

overseas development council   october 1973

The views expressed in this monograph are those of the author, and do not necessarily represent those of the Overseas Development Council, its directors, officers, or staff.

foreword

Major changes in our relations with the rest of the world during the past two years have dramatized a period of transition in U.S. foreign policy. The long-standing confrontation between the two major superpowers has waned, and the President of the United States has been feted in both Moscow and Peking. The conflict in Southeast Asia which many saw as the culmination of this ideological confrontation is winding down, and U.S. troops have been withdrawn from that war-torn peninsula.

However, the "new era" of U.S. foreign relations that these changes symbolize is also marked by new problems that will pose great difficulties for Americans whether they are policy makers or interested citizens. Most Americans have been dismayed by the apparent vulnerability of the U.S. economy in recent months. The sacrosanct dollar has been devalued twice, travel has become more expensive, food prices have skyrocketed, and gas and fuel oil are in short supply.

The current "energy crisis," for instance, seems a precursor of a growing global shortage of raw materials. The Secretary of the Interior estimates that by the end of the century we will have to import more than half of our supplies of all but one of the fifteen principal raw materials needed for American industry. In large measure, these resources are controlled by the developing countries. Likewise, we are beginning to understand the growing dimensions of global interdependence in trying to find solutions for emerging problems such as preserving our own environment, controlling the narcotics trade, sharing the resources of the seas, shaping the potential of burgeoning technology, and assessing the implications of the multinational corporations. In all of these areas, Americans will find that they have to deal on the basis of increasing equality with a much greater number of countries, many of which fall into the category of developing. In effect, the new international systems that we need will not work well for any one country unless they work well for all.

The United States faces certain challenges in responding to this changing situation. We can seek new modes of collaboration among countries, or we can retreat into sterile autarky and a world marked more by confrontation than by collaboration. So far the U.S. response has been fragmentary and parochial. It has centered on attempts to create a new balance between the major power centers of the world while almost totally ignoring the needs and objectives of the developing countries. In effect, current United States foreign policy pays much less attention today than ten years ago to the three quarters of the inhabitants of this globe who face deep and continuing problems of poverty, malnutrition, disease, and illiteracy.

This current disinterest of the Legislative and Executive branches of the American government in responding to the needs of the poor countries is quite apparent. In the case of bilateral development assistance, the United States, which pioneered this concept and charged others to do their fair share, is now laggard in this area—ranking fourteenth among the sixteen members of the Development Assistance Committee (DAC) of the OECD in the share of its gross national product provided for development assistance. Although the United States accounts for roughly one half of the GNP of the DAC member countries, its share of GNP devoted to development assistance continues to decline.

Similarly, the United States has ignored the needs and objectives of the poor countries in the negotiations which seek to restructure the international monetary system. It was also less forthcoming than most developed countries in addressing the requests made by the poor countries at the United Nations Trade and Development Conference held in Santiago, Chile, in 1972. Other actions illustrate the same decline in U.S. interest. Moreover, in recent years, our traditional leadership in supporting international organizations such as the United Nations Development Programme and the World Bank's International Development Association has waned; in the conspicuous cases of IDA and the Asian Development Bank, we are even laggard in meeting our funding commitments.

What do Americans think of this trend in U.S. policy? We know that during the "cold war" period public opinion supported the main lines of United States foreign policy. There was "agreement on the main themes of contemporary foreign policy—resistance to communist expansion by economic, diplomatic, propaganda, and, if necessary, military means, and the establishment of a peaceful and legal international order in which American material and security interests would be protected."[1] This consensus governed all facets of United States foreign policy for twenty years after 1945 and was particularly strong in the case of American policies toward the two thirds of the world considered to be "underdeveloped." But what do Americans believe now, nearly three decades after the end of World War II? Are they still concerned and sympathetic about the problems of development and the plight of people in the developing countries? Or has the

[1] Gabriel A. Almond, *American People and Foreign Policy* (New York: Praeger Publishers, 1950), pp. 158-9.

bitter experience of the Vietnamese conflict and the pressing nature of our domestic problems come to predominate the American outlook on the developing world?

In order to answer some of these questions, the Overseas Development Council undertook to survey American attitudes on a wide range of questions involving international poverty and development. In recent years, a great deal of excellent work has been done concerning American attitudes toward foreign policy questions. It has provided a wealth of information on American attitudes on foreign and domestic issues. However, not much has been done to explore American attitudes on global poverty and development or on U.S. relations with the developing countries—except for surveys focusing solely on the U.S. foreign aid program. It is not very surprising that many Americans want to cut budgetary allocations for foreign aid, in view of domestic needs and of the fact that the public is quite ignorant of the size of the U.S. aid effort both in absolute terms and in relation to the programs of other developed countries. But this predictable response does not give much of an indication of how Americans would respond— especially if better informed—to new and different policies aimed   v at attacking international poverty. The Overseas Development Council therefore undertook the survey in order to find out what Americans know about these issues, what their attitudes are toward the problems of poor countries, and finally, where they get their information on the developing countries. The results are analyzed in this monograph and provide a wealth of useful information.

The survey's findings should have utility for several different audiences. They provide a road map to be used by all those concerned with United States relationships with the developing countries and with United States foreign policy in general. For the policy maker and analyst of American attitudes on foreign policy, the survey results will present a good overview of an area of public opinion that has never yet been explored. As Bernard Cohen has pointed out, "public opinion very rarely comes to foreign policy unambiguously or uniformly as the public presumes; it comes rather in small bits and pieces; on all sides of issues; on no side of them; even on non-issues; and serious substantive policy-related responsiveness to such a mixed and contradictory bag is often beyond the reach of mortal man."[2] Some of the ambiguities and contradictions should be resolved by this survey.

For those outside of government who are interested in strengthening U.S. support for the development of the poor countries, the survey's findings give some indication of how American public opinion can be mobilized in favor of a more positive set of U.S. development policies and programs. For those within the U.S. government who wish to increase public concern about U.S. relations with the underdeveloped countries, the survey provides insights about the kinds of policy and program changes required to win wider public support.

---

[2]Bernard C. Cohen, *The Public's Impact on Foreign Policy* (Boston: Little, Brown and Company, 1973), p. 194.

This survey originated when we at the Overseas Development Council were approached by the U.S. Coalition for Development, an organization of youth groups interested in programs of development education, for assistance in undertaking a survey of youth attitudes. We agreed to undertake a parallel survey of attitudes of the general populace in the hope that the two together would give policy makers and others the first comprehensive picture of American opinion on a range of issues facing the United States and the poor countries. The survey's results, analyzed in this monograph, are to be made available to as wide an audience as possible. We also hope that other groups will use the questions to measure the opinions of their members on the local level.

The Council gratefully acknowledges the support given this project by a number of organizations and individuals. The youth survey was given initial support by a grant from the U.N. Centre for Economic and Social Information (CESI), as well as from the Chase Manhattan Bank Foundation and the International Business Machines Corporation. The general survey was financed by the Overseas Development Council, with the help of a grant from the Edna McConnell Clark Foundation. The survey itself was carried out by Peter D. Hart Associates, a survey firm located in Washington. We owe much to the advice and help of Peter Hart and his former colleague, David Cooper, who conducted the survey and with whom we worked closely in designing the questionnaire.

We at the ODC are issuing this survey in the hope that it will provide for those interested in U.S. relations with the poor countries a clearer picture of the attitudes and opinions of their fellow countrymen. In the past, Americans have been willing to be helpful toward other nations and other peoples—particularly when it has appeared to be in their enlightened interest. This survey indicates that the concern on which this earlier assistance support was based still exists. Therefore, it is up to those interested in public policy to begin the programs of public education and discussion necessary to inform their fellow citizens of the changes in the international environment in which we all will be living in the years to come. Likewise, it is up to policy makers to make those changes in policies and programs which will both strengthen the efficacy of these programs and enhance their public acceptance.

John W. Sewell, *Vice President*
Overseas Development Council

October 1973

vi

acknowledgments

This national public opinion study has been a joint effort since its genesis. The United States Coalition for Development (USCD)— five youth organizations concerned with global poverty issues—is largely responsible for this survey project's beginning. Paul D. Schaeffer, former Executive Director of the USCD, deserves credit for helping to initiate, organize, and monitor the project. The author is grateful to Alfred O. Hero, Jr., World Peace Foundation Director and an expert in the field of public opinion analysis, for his generous comments at various phases of this project. The author also wishes to thank Martha Mills, Charles Dennison, and Steven Kidd for their comments on the survey manuscript.

John W. Sewell, ODC Vice President, provided conceptual advice during this eighteen-month project, and contributed the government policy recommendations in the final section of Chapter VII. ODC Research Assistant Malcolm Russell was indefatigable in helping analyze the survey data. Thanks are also due to ODC's Executive Editor, Valeriana Kallab, and Rosemarie Philips, Editorial Assistant, for shaping the survey findings for publication. Finally, the critical comments and encouragement of my colleague and wife Susan were an essential ingredient to this survey project's completion.

Paul A. Laudicina, *Associate Fellow*
Overseas Development Council

October 1973

table of contents

introduction

There appears to be no dearth of information regarding American attitudes on almost any issue. Public opinion on domestic political programs, tax issues, budgetary priorities, war and peace, U.S.-Soviet relations, toothpaste preferences, and countless other matters has been explored time and again. One would expect, then, that American attitudes concerning U.S. relations with the people and nations of Asia, Africa, and Latin America—together comprising about three fourths of the globe's population—had been similarly examined. Yet this is not so. Some U.S. public opinion analysts have been quick to respond by citing survey after survey on the American public's views on foreign assistance as relevant evidence. But the public has so many perceptions and misperceptions of foreign aid that it would be highly misleading to use popular support or opposition to aid *alone* as a barometer of public attitudes on global poverty and development issues.

Other nations, however, have sponsored in-depth analyses of development attitudes. A survey conducted by the British government during 1969 showed widespread, though superficial, British sympathy with the peoples and problems of the developing world.[1] Similarly, a 1968 Swedish survey revealed a limited public knowledge and interest in underdeveloped nations based upon feelings of humanitarianism and human solidarity.[2] Prior to this survey, however, U.S. public opinion research had not explored American attitudes on poverty and development questions beyond those specifically relating to the U.S. foreign aid program.[3]

---

[1]I. Rauta, *Aid and Overseas Development: A Survey of Public Attitudes, Opinions and Knowledge* (London: Her Majesty's Stationery Office, 1971).

[2]Stig Lindholm, *The Image of the Developing Countries: An Inquiry into Swedish Public Opinion* (Uppsala, Sweden: The Dag Hammarskjold Foundation, 1971).

[3]The most comprehensive of these earlier analyses of public positions on foreign assistance questions is Alfred O. Hero, Jr., "Foreign Aid and the American Public," *Public Policy*, Vol. 14 (1965), pp. 71-116. This study summarizes American opinions on aid from the late 1940s through 1965.

What do Americans think of poor people and poverty? Why are people, and countries, poor? Can these conditions be changed? How? What should we as individuals and as a nation do to change world conditions? Surely no simple examination of the public's perceptions of foreign aid programs alone can provide answers to such questions. One problem in looking for answers to these questions is that everyone to some extent claims to be his own public opinion analyst, and holds certain theories and assumptions about what the public knows, believes, fears, supports, or opposes.

One such assumption currently in vogue among foreign policy observers in particular is that a new mood of isolationism has settled in among Americans, precluding any active U.S. public concern with international problems. Since the beginning of the public reaction against continuation of the Vietnam war, it has been widely claimed—more on the basis of intuitive appraisal than actual survey data—that the American public has "had enough." From negative responses to questions such as whether or not the United States should intervene militarily in the Middle East if Israel is threatened, or from positive responses to questions such as whether Americans should remain independent in world affairs, some foreign policy observers have concluded that Americans are opposed to *any* active expression of international concern. The data do indicate that Americans will not tolerate more military engagements of the Vietnam order. But to conclude that this equals neo-isolationism is leap-frog logic. There is, after all, a range of foreign policy alternatives between Vietnam and Fortress America.

At a time when official U.S. support for international development efforts has apparently reached its nadir, the question of whether or not the American people approve of this trend is obviously important. Since the end of World War II, the United States has assumed a leading role in orchestrating a global effort to attack world poverty. It seems obvious that if this effort is not to deteriorate further, or indeed, if it is to be strengthened, the United States must remain a major participant. At the moment, however, there are no clear indications of what foreign policies the American public will support. Clearly, the public ranks domestic priorities higher than international issues, and there is growing support to cut back on military expenditures. But do Americans have some perception of the vast changes now taking place in relations between states? And will they support the kinds of forthcoming American policies that are needed to deal with these changes?

Questions such as these make what Americans think, as well as know, about global poverty and development of crucial importance. Does the public approve of the decline in U.S. government support for developing countries? Do Americans know what the dimensions of development problems are and what is being done to solve them? Do Americans really care about the problems which developing nations and poor people everywhere face? If so, who are these Americans? How can these people be reached? What sources of information determine their opinions on development and poverty issues?

These questions guided the design of our survey questionnaire. A group of experienced public opinion analysts, community organizers, and development educators was consulted on the content of the questionnaire in the early stages of the survey project. This group's independent advice on both the substance and form of the survey proved invaluable throughout the project's course. Six "focus sessions" were organized in a number of U.S. cities. These "freewheeling" development discussions with a small random sample of Americans were also an important tool in formulating the questionnaire, which was then revised and refined numerous times by the Overseas Development Council, the U.S. Coalition for Development,[4] and the survey advisory group. A draft questionnaire was pre-tested by interviewers in the northeastern, southeastern, and western United States.

It was decided that the survey should not rely exclusively on multiple choice questions. Nearly half of the inquiries therefore were designed to be "open-ended"—with no multiple choices offered and responses freely given and recorded. This form of questioning lessens the chance of "leading" or predisposing respondents to answer questions in some particular way. The open-ended approach was an important aspect of the questionnaire design, especially since this survey attempted to probe more deeply into American opinions, emotions, and attitudes rather than to gauge specific knowledge levels on various issues.

Special care was given to the terminology used in the questions. For example, the focus group sessions and numerous questionnaire pre-tests indicated that the most familiar yet unprejudicial description of the countries on which the questioning focused was "underdeveloped countries." Terms such as "third world" or "poor countries" were consciously avoided, since the pre-testing indicated that such terms were either not understood or had emotive connotations.

A sampling expert then prepared the survey's nationwide sample, with a base of 1,200 respondents each for the youth and general populace samples. In the selection of the sample, a stratification technique was applied to 1970 census data to ensure that the cross-section of the public would be proportionately representative not only on a geographic basis but also by size of community.[5] Interviews lasted from forty-five minutes to one and one half hours, averaging just over one hour per interview.

3

---

[4]The U.S. Coalition for Development—sponsor of the youth attitudes portion of this study—consists of the following five youth and student organizations concerned with development: Young World Development, the Student Advisory Committee on International Affairs, the Student and Young Adult Division of the United Nations Association, the U.S. Committee for UNICEF, and the U.S. Youth Council.

[5]For a more complete description of the sample methodology, see Annex B, pp. 115-19. The sample was interviewed nationally between October 12 and October 22, 1972. Interviewers were given explicit instructions on the selection of respondents and the handling of the questionnaire. When a selected respondent was not at home, the interviewer made an appointment to return at a different time. Up to two return calls were made to homes where there initially was no answer.

It is important to note that the purpose of the survey was not to determine exact percentage counts of how very narrowly defined groups of Americans react to, or think about, specific issues—although, in many cases, the evidence justifies such an analysis.[6] Rather, it was our purpose to learn in broad terms what Americans think about global poverty and development, how well informed they are on international development issues, what sources of information they rely upon to form their opinions, and how they are predisposed toward helping to ameliorate the problems of the developing world. We wished to learn what percentage of the public sympathizes with ongoing international development efforts, as well as which groups oppose such attempts to alleviate world poverty. We also sought to identify that segment of the American public which is uncommitted and ambivalent about such issues.

What were the survey results? What do Americans think about poverty and development issues? A twelve-point summary of the survey's findings follows.

4

SUMMARY OF FINDINGS

1. *Americans are generally very ignorant of development issues.* The public appears to understand neither the immensity and character of global poverty problems, nor the limits of the U.S. response, or the prospects for solutions to development problems.

2. Despite this lack of information, *public support for the idea of giving U.S. assistance to underdeveloped countries is at an historic high of 68 per cent*, considerably above the 51 per cent and 58 per cent levels recorded, respectively, in 1958 and 1966. Public opinion on development and aid questions appears to be quite independent of attitudes about the Vietnam war.

3. *One of every three (38 per cent) Americans is basically sympathetic to the concerns of the poor countries. Another 37 per cent of the public is uncommitted and ambivalent, but not negatively predisposed, toward helping these countries. Twenty-five per cent of the public is generally unsympathetic to poor-country needs.*

4. *Development support is more concentrated among young, better-educated, upper-income, and politically liberal Americans.* Yet blacks, too, are potentially strong development supporters, despite their economic and educational position, and young Americans between the ages of eighteen and twenty-five are a potential bulwark of development support.

5. *Americans generally give the solution of domestic problems priority over that of international problems*, despite the fact that the public regards hunger and poverty as very serious world problems deserving of top priority attention. There is considerably more optimism about the feasibility of solving U.S. poverty problems compared to solving those of the developing countries. This optimism concerning the potential for more effective and rapid change at home—coupled with a sense of the more direct conse-

---

[6]Annex C should be consulted for standard statistical sampling error tables, which may be used in the study of this survey data.

quences of, and responsibility for, U.S. poverty—helps account for the public's preoccupation with domestic needs.

6. *Americans clearly favor aiding the poor countries for primarily moral and humanitarian reasons.* The "cold war" rationale for providing economic assistance appears to have lost much of its earlier public acceptance. The public believes that those countries most in need of U.S. economic assistance should be favored in the allocation of such assistance.

7. *While the public expresses a definite sense that U.S. assistance to underdeveloped countries also benefits the United States, Americans are vague as to just what the benefits are.* The public is almost totally unaware of any economic interdependence arguments that make assistance to underdeveloped countries a long-run interest of the United States as well.

8. *The expressed public support for the principle of U.S. assistance for the poor countries is not necessarily translatable into support for U.S. government aid programs.* The American public thinks that too much U.S. official aid is wasted in our own bureaucracy, and that U.S. aid does not get to those who need it most in the poor countries. Americans also question the honesty and integrity of the aid bureaucracies of some recipient governments. The public appears to consider voluntary agencies more reliable assistance channels than government aid programs.

9. *A majority of Americans favor cutting the foreign military assistance budget, and one out of two regards the U.S. provision of military training and equipment as an ineffective and unacceptable form of foreign aid.*

10. *Public support is strongest to alleviate such basic problems as hunger and malnutrition, disease, and illiteracy.* Americans consider aid in these areas to be more direct, its results more visible, and its dispensation less likely to meet with corruption. The public also appears to expect such forms of assistance to do more to strengthen the self-sufficiency of the recipient countries.

11. *Two out of three Americans favor a freer U.S. trade policy with underdeveloped countries as an inducement to the development of those countries, if adequate adjustment assistance provisions are written into U.S. trade legislation.*

12. *Television is the American mass public's single most important source of information on world problems.* Newspapers remain an important communication medium on world problems— especially to better educated Americans. Conferences, pamphlets, and the churches are insignificant sources of development information for the mass public audience.

poverty, development, and the u.s. budget

6   To examine American attitudes on development and poverty in the context of respondents' overall world views, the survey interview began with a few general multiple choice questions about world peace and prosperity. Individual perceptions of the state of the world—and prospects for world economic development—proved to be very subjective, often seeming as bleak or promising as personal economic fears and hopes.

The responses to two questions about world tensions and material conditions showed the mood of most Americans to be optimistic regarding living conditions in the world, and generally pessimistic regarding global tensions. Respondents of all age groups regard the contemporary world scene as more tense than ten years ago, but older people appear to be slightly more optimistic concerning what the conditions of world tension will be in 1982. Blue-collar workers, lower-income groups, black Americans, and individuals with less than a high-school education are considerably more pessimistic about world conditions than are better educated, higher-paid Americans.[1]

Respondents were asked to compare living conditions in the world today with conditions ten years ago and the world standard of living anticipated in ten years. These results indicate that a majority of Americans (63 per cent) believe that world living conditions today are definitely better than ten years ago, and that nearly half of the total national sample (49 per cent) agrees that living conditions ten years from now will be better yet. However, in the case of this question, too, responses indicate a close link between people's attitudes toward the world and their perceptions

---

[1]This relationship between individual income and perception of world standards of living was also evident in response to similar questions asked in previous U.S. surveys. See, for example, Albert H. Cantril and Charles W. Roll, Jr., *Hopes and Fears of the American People* (New York: Universe Books, 1971), p. 78.

Table II-1. Perception of World Tensions Ten Years Ago and Ten Years from Now

	World Tensions Are/Will Be	
	Greater Than 10 Years Ago	Greater 10 Years From Now
Total	67%	38%
Age		
18-25	65	40
26-35	71	43
36-50	60	35
Over 50	71	35
Occupation		
Professional/Executive	56	30
White Collar	65	34
Blue Collar	73	43
Education		
College Graduates	55	26
Some College	62	40
High School Graduates	70	36
Non-High School Graduates	74	45
Income		
Upper	55	31
Middle	68	38
Lower	74	43
Blacks	71	52

Table II-2. Perception of World Living Conditions Ten Years Ago and Ten Years from Now

	World Living Conditions Are/Will Be	
	Better Than 10 Years Ago	Better 10 Years From Now
Total	63%	49%
Age		
18-25	59	54
26-35	64	55
36-50	63	49
Over 50	63	40
Occupation		
Professional/Executive	67	54
White Collar	62	57
Blue Collar	61	44
Education		
College Graduates	69	58
Some College	59	53
High School Graduates	66	52
Non-High School Graduates	57	37
Income		
Upper	66	54
Middle	65	50
Lower	59	43
Blacks	67	51

of their own economic and social positions.[2] Blue-collar and lower-income Americans, as well as those with little formal education, are least convinced that living conditions in the world have improved over the past decade or that things are likely to get much better. In contrast, blacks generally believe that living conditions are better today, and they are more optimistic about conditions ten years hence.

POVERTY

Respondents were also asked whether or not they believed poverty could be eliminated in the United States within the next fifty years and whether or not they believed it could be eliminated in the world during the same period. While there was some optimism among respondents (38 per cent) that poverty could be eliminated over the next fifty years within the United States, most of those questioned (56 per cent) disagreed. Young people (eighteen to twenty-five years old), however, showed greater optimism concerning solutions to domestic poverty problems; almost half of this group of respondents (46 per cent) believed that domestic poverty could be eliminated within fifty years.

Table II-3. Possibility of Eliminating Poverty in the United States and in the World in Next Fifty Years[a]

	Total	Age			
		18-25	26-35	36-50	Over 50
Poverty Could Be Eliminated					
In U.S.	38%	46%	43%	37%	29%
In World	15	16	15	16	13
Poverty Could Not Be Eliminated					
In U.S.	56	50	51	57	62
In World	76	77	75	77	76

[a]"Not sure" responses omitted from table.

Pessimism concerning the possibility of eliminating *world* poverty is much more prevalent, with three out of four of those interviewed (76 per cent) responding negatively, and only 15 per cent believing that world poverty could be eliminated within the next fifty years. Young and old alike agree that it would be virtually impossible to achieve the same level of prosperity internationally as anticipated domestically.

SERIOUSNESS OF WORLD PROBLEMS

Respondents were next provided with a list of twenty world problems and asked to characterize them as very serious, somewhat serious, or not serious. They were then asked to indicate the two

8

---

[2]The 1969 British Overseas Development Administration public opinion survey notes that "attitudes towards aid were closely related to beliefs about whether life in general 'was better in the past' or 'would be better in the future.'" See I. Rauta, *Aid and Overseas Development: A Survey of Public Attitudes, Opinions and Knowledge* (London: Her Majesty's Stationery Office, 1971), p. 54.

problems which they felt should receive priority attention. Four out of five Americans (80 per cent) considered drug abuse to be a very serious world problem and almost half (46 per cent) ranked this problem as demanding the highest priority. Thus most respondents characterized what is essentially a U.S. or industrialized-country problem—and one that was not even considered a problem ten years ago—as a "world" problem.

Table II-4. List of World Problems Ranked by Respondents According to Relative Seriousness[a]

	Very Serious	Somewhat Serious	Not Serious	Top Priority Problem
Drug Abuse	80%	16%	4%	46%
Hunger & Poverty	71	24	5	41
Using Up Natural Resources	67	26	7	18
Pollution	66	28	6	24
Communism	60	28	12	20
Corrupt Governments	59	32	9	23
Hatred Between Racial & Ethnic Groups	58	34	8	17
Lack of Communication Among People	55	33	12	14
Overpopulation	54	32	14	16
Poor Medical Care	51	36	13	17
Illiteracy	42	42	16	9
Lack of Adequate Housing	41	44	15	7
Religious Wars	41	37	22	5
Corporate Power	38	42	20	3
Territorial Disputes	27	44	29	2
Socialism	27	41	32	4
Capitalism	26	40	34	2
Too Much Automation	22	40	38	2
Trade Barriers	13	47	40	1
Too Much Technology	12	28	60	1

[a]Percentages based on those respondents who had already identified the issues as problems.

The problem viewed as second most serious was hunger and poverty. Nearly three out of four Americans (71 per cent) consider world hunger and poverty to be one of the most serious problems with which we are confronted. Forty-one per cent of the public assigned this problem top priority. More than four out of five (81 per cent) young Americans considered hunger and poverty to be the most serious world problem today. The view that problems of world hunger and poverty are serious and deserving of urgent attention is not unique to U.S. public opinion. The results of a British public opinion survey, for example, singled out hunger and famine as the world problem most deserving of urgent attention.[3]

The problem of trade barriers received no such high priority in the eyes of the American public. Since U.S. trade policy is of paramount importance to the development of the poor countries, the public attitude on this issue is considered in greater detail in Chapter IV of this study.

---

[3]See I. Rauta, *Aid and Overseas Development*, p. 12.

9

THE GAP BETWEEN RICH AND POOR

Respondents were asked if they thought that the gap between the rich and poor people in the United States had widened in the past ten years, was about the same, or was narrower than ten years ago. They were asked to make the same judgment with regard to the gap between rich and poor countries.

Table II-5. Perception of Changes in the Gap Between Rich and Poor People/Countries Over Last Ten Years[a]

	Total	Education			
		College Graduates	Some College	High School Graduates	Non-High School Graduates
Gap Has Widened					
Between rich and poor people in U.S.	34%	34%	36%	34%	34%
Between rich and poor countries	31	40	34	29	26
Gap Has Remained Same					
Between rich and poor people in U.S.	31	30	29	31	33
Between rich and poor countries	33	30	34	34	35
Gap Has Narrowed					
Between rich and poor people in U.S.	28	31	33	29	22
Between rich and poor countries	19	21	21	21	13

[a]"Not sure" responses omitted from table.

The results indicate that Americans have no uniform feeling that the gap between rich and poor people in the United States and between nations is indeed widening; nor are they confident that it is being bridged. In its answers to these two questions, the American public divided fairly evenly among those who believed the gap had widened, those who thought it had remained the same, and those who thought it had narrowed. Clearly the concept of a widening rich-poor gap makes little impression on the public's sense of the urgency of attending to global underdevelopment problems.

WHAT IS DEVELOPMENT?

The word "development" is widely used but rarely explained to the general public. Even for those working in the field of international development it has multiple meanings. It is often taken to mean improvement in economic growth, standards of living, or the general welfare of (primarily) the poor countries of Asia, Africa, and Latin America.

What do Americans understand to be the meaning of "development"? What reactions does the word evoke? Is it the best word, consequently, for educators to use in discussing "development issues"? Answers to our open-ended survey question indicate that Americans generally do understand the word "development"

Table II-6. Definitions of "Development" (open-ended question)[a]

	Total	Education			
		College Graduates	Some College	High School Graduates	Non-High School Graduates
Improving living conditions, raising standard of living	13%	20%	14%	10%	11%
Helping people stand on their own feet, help themselves, self-improvement	12	13	12	14	9
Growth, building things up, getting stronger	12	6	9	13	15
Bettering the human condition, better life for people	9	9	9	8	10
Solving problems, improving a situation, improving what they've got	8	6	4	9	9
Improving education, facilities for schools	8	10	12	10	5
Bringing progress, new ideas	7	5	9	7	6
Improving economic well-being, economic stability	5	10	8	4	3
Bringing in machinery, industry, technology, modernization, increasing productivity	5	8	6	5	3
Improving relationships between countries. Making the world a better place to live	4	6	6	3	4
Improving housing, building new places to live	3	2	2	3	2
Ending wars, bringing peace	3	3	4	2	2
Making the most of what you have, maximizing use of resources	3	6	4	4	1

[a]Totals are less than 100 per cent since responses of 2 per cent or less are not shown.

to refer to concepts of "growth," "building," and "improving." But the fact that not more than 13 per cent of the respondents understand development in any single sense is indicative of the multiple meanings the word has for the public. This diversity is not surprising, in view of the differences among economists and foreign policy analysts themselves over the meanings of development.

Generally, Americans with less education and lower incomes regard development as a process of physical construction, growth, and building. Individuals with more formal education tend to perceive of development in "standard of living" terms. But neither group seems to understand development in very "human" terms; perceptions of the process tend to be vaguely economic. Neither do Americans understand the word "development" to mean libera-

Table II-7. Views on Why Poor People are Poor (open-ended question)[a]

	Total	Education				Income			Blacks
		College Graduates	Some College	High School Graduates	Non-High School Graduates	Upper	Middle	Lower	
Lack of education, ignorance, illiteracy	43%	44%	43%	48%	36%	48%	44%	37%	36%
Lazy, no ambition, no drive, don't get out and work, want to be poor, prefer welfare	40	37	34	44	41	42	43	35	31
Lack of opportunity, never had a chance, can't get decent jobs, don't have equal opportunity	25	26	27	22	25	28	24	24	33
They are born into it, the only life they know, it's environmental, they inherit it	19	29	29	15	13	23	20	16	11
Handicapped, poor health, illness	6	6	3	6	9	5	5	8	4
Don't know how to manage, take care of money, what they have	6	3	4	7	8	5	5	9	3
They are victims of the system, the social structure; government	6	9	8	5	4	8	6	4	7
Not enough job training, no skills	4	6	4	6	4	4	6	4	11
Some are just less fortunate, in the wrong place at the wrong time	3	4	2	1	5	3	2	5	1

[a]Totals do not add up to 100 per cent because respondents could give several answers.

tion or freedom from oppression. They also do not perceive of development in negative terms of *excessive* growth or overconsumption. When asked directly whether they reacted positively or negatively to the word "development," four out of five (79 per cent) Americans stated that they reacted positively, while only 6 per cent considered the word to have negative connotations.

WHY ARE POOR PEOPLE POOR?

The survey also sought to determine American perceptions of why people are poor. In general, the responses showed that Americans appreciate the ways in which "the system" can determine an individual's economic fate. Taken together, the responses to questions concerning the causes of poverty clearly indicate that Americans do comprehend and sympathize with the situation of helplessness facing poor people throughout the world. Over two out of five Americans offered lack of education as the basic reason why people are poor. Almost the same number stated that poor people lack ambition, are lazy, have no drive, prefer welfare to working—in short, that they choose poverty.

13

    Responses to the open-ended question recorded in Table II-7 show that except for the second reason, lack of ambition, Americans believe that people are poor because of factors beyond their control. One in four (25 per cent) believe people are poor because they lack the opportunity to improve their condition. An additional 19 per cent believe that people are born into poverty. Lower-income Americans (earning under $7,000 per year) consider lack of education (37 per cent) and lack of ambition (35 per cent) to be the major factors determining poverty. Black Americans assign relatively greater importance to "lack of opportunity" (33 per cent) and "job training" (11 per cent) as determinants of poverty. The public sees higher education—the great american dream—as a factor important to economic success. The Horatio Alger myth seems operative in the responses to this question of the causes of poverty. Americans do tend to believe "you can make it if you work hard enough for it and if you really want it." Yet, there is considerable sympathy and understanding for the possibility that the "cards may be stacked against you."

WHAT IS AN UNDERDEVELOPED COUNTRY?

Respondents were then asked to describe their understanding of an "underdeveloped country." Since most had already identified education as the most important determining factor in whether or not an individual is poor, it was not surprising that they now expressed the belief that poor educational facilities, illiteracy, and low levels of education are the prime factors accounting for the underdevelopment of countries. While Americans respond quickly to the short-term, dramatic, and immediate needs of the poor countries resulting from famine, disease, and natural disaster, these are not the basic causes of underdevelopment in the view of the public. Rather, attention to the educational needs of the developing world appeals to the public as an important, long-term solution for development problems.

Table II-8. Definitions of "Underdeveloped Country" (open-ended question)[a]

	Total	College Graduates	Some College	High School Graduates	Non-High School Graduates
			Education		
Poor educational facilities, undereducated, illiterate	40%	47%	44%	40%	31%
Not enough technology, manufacturing, industry. No exports for trade	24	30	27	23	22
Poor economy, low standard of living, poverty stricken	20	22	24	18	17
Can't feed their own people, hunger	19	22	24	18	15
Limited natural resources, poor land, no tools	12	12	14	14	7
Bad housing	12	14	9	14	11
Poor government, unstable governments that exploit	12	18	13	10	9
Do not use their resources to the fullest, do not work up to their potential	11	23	13	11	5
Poor medical facilities, much illness, disease, high mortality	10	16	13	11	6
Overpopulation, too many people, families too large	9	13	13	9	4
Bad living conditions, sub-standard conditions	7	6	7	7	8
The people are unaware, do not have the know-how	7	7	7	7	9
A country that is not developed	4	2	3	4	4

[a]Totals do not add up to 100 per cent because respondents could give several answers.

Forty per cent of the respondents considered illiteracy to be the basic attribute of an underdeveloped country. The "lack of technology, manufacturing, and basic industry," as well as the "absence of exports for trade," were offered as descriptive of an underdeveloped country by 24 per cent of the respondents.[4] An almost equal number of people (20 per cent) stated that an underdeveloped country is one with a "poor economy" and "low standard of living," where "people are hungry." Only 11 per cent of the national sample offered a reason that seemed to fault the people of underdeveloped countries with their own underdevelopment by stating that "they do not use their resources to the fullest, and do not work up to their potential."

[4]In response to a similar question asked in the recent British survey, the British public understood the term "underdeveloped country" to have nearly the same meaning that Americans ascribed to it. Americans, however, gave the lack of manufacturing and technology greater importance in the explanation of an underdeveloped country than did the English who emphasized food scarcity and poor agriculture. See I. Rauta, *Aid and Overseas Development*, p. 36.

14

U.S. BUDGET PRIORITIES

If Americans perceive of hunger and poverty as a serious world problem and assign high priority to the solution of this problem, what sort of budgetary emphasis would they give poverty-related programs? American reactions to budgetary priorities are, of course, a reflection of policy preferences. As such, these survey questions are of considerable importance. An examination of the responses to the next two questions makes it apparent that Americans are mainly interested in allocating U.S. tax dollars for the solution of *domestic* problems.

Respondents were provided with a list of U.S. budgetary items and outlays for 1973 and asked whether they would in each case favor increasing the budget, keeping it the same, or cutting it.

Table II-9. Views on Allocation of U. S. Budget

	Total	Age			
		18-25	26-35	36-50	Over 50
Budget Items Respondents Felt Should Be Increased					
Education	68%	83%	75%	67%	53%
Pollution Control	65	81	67	62	54
Medical Services	51	59	55	47	47
Social Security	50	49	55	48	51
Budget Items Respondents Felt Should Be Kept the Same					
National Defense	46	36	41	46	55
Economic Assistance to Foreign Countries[a]	41	45	36	44	42
Food Stamps	40	38	41	40	42
Farm Price Supports	38	38	39	34	41
Budget Items Respondents Felt Should Be Decreased					
Military Assistance to Foreign Countries	52	53	52	54	47
Economic Assistance to Foreign Countries[a]	43	29	49	44	47
Space Research	44	35	42	42	55

[a]Economic assistance to foreign countries is included in two categories since approximately equal numbers of respondents favored cutting the economic assistance budget as keeping it the same.

The four items most Americans chose to increase were, in order of priority: education, pollution control, medical services, and social security. Fifty per cent or more of all Americans favor increased budget allotments for each of these items. Increases in social security are favored by Americans of all ages, while additional funds for education and environmental programs are favored heavily by young Americans. The public feels that U.S. budget allocations should be maintained at present spending levels for national defense, economic assistance to foreign countries, food stamps, and farm price supports. The three items which Americans believe could be cut back are military assistance to foreign countries, economic assistance to foreign countries, and space research. (Economic assistance is included in both of the last two categories since approximately equal numbers of respondents favored cutting this budget item as favored keeping it the same.) Older Americans are much more supportive of cuts in economic aid to foreign countries than are young Americans—as is shown in Table II-9. Although the public considers world poverty a problem deserving high priority attention and is basically in favor of the idea of U.S. foreign assistance—as will be shown in the next chapter—43 per cent (especially older Americans) favors decreasing U.S. budget allocations for foreign economic assistance.

This seeming contradiction also appears in European survey data. While 42 per cent of all Englishmen consider that Britain should maintain or increase its foreign aid budget, 86 per cent believe that the government should attend to domestic poverty before giving money to other countries.[5] Like the public in most other countries, Americans believe that domestic problems and priorities should have first call upon tax revenue.[6] This probably is not so much an ethnocentric phenomenon as it is a belief that money spent abroad is often wasted or not efficaciously applied to development problems—a subject to which we will return later in this study. Global poverty problems and their possible solutions are more remote from the consciousness of most Americans than are domestic needs. Therefore, since most Americans do not easily conceive of global poverty problems, they are less willing to spend tax revenue on attempts to solve them. The responses, of course, also reflect a feeling that "charity begins at home."

TOTAL U.S. EXPENDITURES ON POVERTY

Respondents were asked to indicate which statement of four they preferred regarding the specific allocation of the portion of the U.S. budget used to fight hunger and poverty at home and abroad. More than half (55 per cent) indicated that most of these U.S. allocations should go for domestic programs and only a small portion for poverty programs abroad. More college graduates and upper-income Americans hold this opinion than do others. One out of every six persons (18 per cent) believes that total U.S. poverty expenditures should be divided more nearly on a fifty-fifty basis. Only 6 per cent of the public feels that U.S. total expenditures on poverty should be divided between domestic programs and foreign assistance according to need—with most of the money thus going to help the poor in other parts of the world. The responses, in effect, support the current, preponderantly domestic distribution of U.S. total poverty expenditures.

Respondents were then asked: "If you were told that 95 per cent of the poor people in the world lived in other countries and the United States had only 5 per cent of the world's poor, would you reconsider your distribution of money?"[7] Twenty-six per

---

[5] I. Rauta, *Aid and Overseas Development*, pp. 20 and 26.

[6] *Ibid.*, and Stig Lindholm, *The Image of the Developing Countries: An Inquiry into Swedish Public Opinion* (Uppsala, Sweden: The Dag Hammarskjold Foundation, 1971), p. 43.

[7] While there is no internationally accepted definition of what constitutes poverty, the hypothesis of 95 per cent is, by any standard, an underestimate of the percentage of the world's poor living outside the United States.

Table II-10. Allocation of Total U.S. Expenditures on Poverty (Domestic and International)

	Total	Education				Age				Income			Blacks
		College Graduates	Some College	High School Graduates	Non-High School Graduates	18-25	26-35	36-50	Over 50	Upper	Middle	Lower	
The total budget should be used for domestic poverty.	13%	6%	11%	13%	15%	10%	12%	13%	16%	8%	12%	17%	14%
A small percentage of the budget should be used to fight poverty in other parts of the world.	55	63	58	57	47	54	56	54	55	61	54	52	47
The budget should be divided about fifty-fifty between the poor of the U. S. and the poor in other parts of the world.	18	21	20	15	21	22	17	20	15	19	21	16	21
The budget should be divided proportionally so that most of it would go to help the poor in other parts of the world.	6	5	6	6	6	7	5	5	6	8	6	5	6
Not sure	8	5	5	9	11	7	10	8	8	4	7	10	12

Table II-11. Willingness of Respondents to Reconsider Allocation of Total U.S. Poverty Expenditures

Would Reconsider	26%
Would Not Reconsider	59%
Not Sure	15%

cent of the respondents said they would reconsider; of these 34 per cent would divide the poverty budget so that *half* would go to helping the poor in other parts of the world, while 53 per cent would actually divide it so that *most* would go to helping the poor in other parts of the world. This shift indicates that, provided with certain facts, 40 per cent of the public would favor earmarking at least half of total U.S. poverty expenditures to help the poor in other nations. In answering the previous, unconditioned question, only 24 per cent of the sample favored such a distribution of funds. This shift suggests that if Americans were better informed regarding the scale of overseas poverty, considerably more public support could be expected for increasing U.S. international poverty allocations. International priorities could gain much stronger support among the American public if educational campaigns impressed upon Americans the magnitude of the problems and the need for a vigorous response. However, this in no sense mitigates the data demonstrating that Americans definitely consider domestic priorities to be of the first importance.

HOW MUCH HELP IS NEEDED BY UNDERDEVELOPED COUNTRIES?

In considering the level of assistance to the poor countries that the public will support, it is obviously important to understand how much assistance Americans believe underdeveloped countries need. Respondents were asked to select from among four statements the one closest to their own view. Fifty per cent of the public believes that developing countries need only a little help from the outside to get to the point of self-sufficiency, whereas almost a third (30 per cent) believes that the poor countries will need a great deal of help for a long time. While few (6 per cent) feel that the underdeveloped countries can succeed on their own, an almost equally small number (9 per cent) believe that these countries will be dependent forever. Thus while Americans are realistic as to the need for help, they are not overly pessimistic as to the prospects for the economic independence of the poor countries. (See Table II-13.)

U.S. GOVERNMENT COMMITMENT

Finally, respondents were asked if they believed that the U.S. government was now doing (a) more, (b) about the right amount, or (c) less than it should to fight domestic or world poverty. Here the public's emphasis upon domestic priorities is once again evident. Only 13 per cent of the respondents feel that the U.S. government is doing more than it should to fight *domestic* poverty,

18

Table II-12. Views on Allocation of Total U.S. Expenditures on Poverty Before and After 26 Per Cent Reconsidered

	Before Reconsidering[a]		After Reconsidering	
	Total Responses	26 Per Cent	26 Per Cent	Total Responses[a]
The total budget should be used for domestic poverty.	13%	14%	4%	10%
A small percentage of the budget should be used to fight poverty in other parts of the world.	55	58	9	42
The budget should be divided about fifty-fifty between the poor of the United States and the poor in other parts of the world.	18	27	34	20
The budget should be divided proportionally so that most of it would go to help the poor in other parts of the world.	6	1	53	20

[a]Eight per cent were "not sure" how they would divide the poverty budget.

19

Table II-13. Views on Help Needed By Underdeveloped Countries

	Total	Education				Age				Income		
		College Graduates	Some College	High School Graduates	Non-High School Graduates	18-25	26-35	36-50	Over 50	Upper	Middle	Lower
Underdeveloped countries can make it on their own without help from the outside.	6%	4%	5%	5%	8%	5%	6%	5%	6%	4%	5%	7%
Underdeveloped countries need a little help from the outside to get to the point when they can stand on their own.	50	41	47	53	51	52	51	50	48	45	51	53
Underdeveloped countries will need a great deal of help for a long time before they can become self-sufficient.	30	49	37	29	19	34	31	32	26	43	31	22
No matter how much help underdeveloped countries are given, they will never be able to make it without help from the outside.	9	4	9	9	13	7	9	8	13	6	10	9
Not Sure	5	2	2	4	9	2	3	5	7	2	3	9

while 44 per cent believe that the U.S. government is doing more than it should to fight *world* poverty. Over half of the American public (54 per cent) feels that the U.S. government is doing less than it should to fight *domestic* poverty, whereas only 17 per cent feels that governmental support for programs aimed at *world* poverty is less than it should be.

Table II-14. Attitudes on Whether U.S. Government Is Doing More or Less Than It Should to Fight Domestic and World Poverty

| | U.S. Doing More Than It Should | | U.S. Doing Less Than It Should | |
	Domestic Poverty	World Poverty	Domestic Poverty	World Poverty
Total	13%	44%	54%	17%
Age				
18-25	7	36	72	27
26-35	14	51	61	15
36-50	16	41	51	16
Over 50	15	46	37	12
Occupation				
Professional/Executive	12	41	61	22
White Collar	12	44	56	18
Blue Collar	13	46	55	16
Income				
Upper	13	41	59	21
Middle	14	48	56	17
Lower	11	40	47	14
Blacks	9	35	60	19

21

It is significant that while 44 per cent of the public believes that the United States is doing "more" than it should to fight world poverty, a mere 2 per cent is actually aware of the fact that the U.S. economic foreign assistance budget is *relatively less* (in share of GNP terms) than foreign assistance programs of other wealthy countries. In fact, an overwhelming 69 per cent thinks that the U.S. foreign assistance budget is greater than those of other countries. More than half (55 per cent) of the public believes that our aid budget should be equal to those of other industrialized countries in relative terms. Some 20 per cent of the survey respondents favor a U.S. aid budget larger than those of other countries, while only 12 per cent think the American aid budget should be relatively less than those of other rich countries. In response to other questions on this subject, 57 per cent of the American public thought that the United States could not afford to give assistance—as did 76 per cent of all Englishmen in the British survey. Yet, more Americans (84 per cent) said that their government was doing its fair share for the poor countries than did Englishmen (67 per cent).[8]

The above data are consistent with the survey's findings regarding the relative ignorance of Americans on aid questions, as will be discussed in the next chapter. The responses suggest that if

[8]I. Rauta, *Aid and Overseas Development*, p. 41.

the American public were aware of the fact that the United States now ranks fourteenth among sixteen major aid donors in official development assistance, the prospects for developing support for increasing U.S. aid probably would be considerably enhanced.

PERSONAL AND VOLUNTARY COMMITMENT

Answers to a further series of questions contrast the American people's understanding of the commitment of the U.S. government with their own commitment to solving problems of hunger and poverty. While four out of five Americans (80 per cent) feel that the government's commitment is fairly strong or very strong, only 63 per cent feel that their own commitment is equally strong.

Table II-15. Comparison of Personal and U.S. Government Commitment
to Solving Problems of Hunger and Poverty

	Personal Commitment				U.S. Commitment			
	Very Strong	Fairly Strong	Not Strong	Not Sure	Very Strong	Fairly Strong	Not Strong	Not Sure
Total	20%	43%	32%	5%	31%	49%	15%	5%
18-25 years	15	43	39	3	22	57	19	2
26-35 years	24	39	34	3	31	48	15	6
36-50 years	21	42	31	6	32	49	15	4
Over 50 years	20	46	26	8	36	46	10	8

Nearly one in three (31 per cent) believes the U.S. commitment to be very strong, while only 20 per cent consider their own commitment to be as strong. This pattern cuts across all age groupings. Nearly one third (32 per cent) of all the respondents feel that their own commitment is not strong at all. Younger respondents also perceive themselves to be primarily uninvolved with hunger and poverty problems. This probably reflects a feeling among young people that they ought to be more strongly devoted to solving poverty problems when in fact, by national standards, they are relatively highly committed already.

When respondents were asked how much they felt people like themselves were committed to helping to solve problems of hunger and poverty, it became evident that they believed the involvement of their neighbors to be equally weak. Only 14 per cent of the sample felt that people like themselves were doing all that they could, 30 per cent felt they were doing less than expected, and another 13 per cent said they were doing nothing at all to help solve problems of hunger and poverty. Younger and upper-income Americans tended to be more critical; older and lower-income individuals were less distressed about the lack of commitment of people like themselves.

Seventeen per cent of the respondents said that they had, at some time, worked as volunteers for organizations that help people in underdeveloped countries. The percentages of those who would be more willing to help government organizations and of those who would be more willing to help private organizations were the same (34 per cent). Of the respondents with relatively more formal education, professionals, and young people—that is,

Table II-16. Volunteering Spare Time to Help People in Underdeveloped Countries

	Total	Education				Profession			Age				Sex	
		College Graduates	Some College	High School Graduates	Non-High School Graduates	Professional/ Executive	White Collar	Blue Collar	18-25	26-35	36-50	Over 50	Male	Female
Have Volunteered In Past	17%	25%	22%	16%	13%	22%	17%	13%	19%	16%	17%	17%	14%	20%
Kind Of Organization Prefer														
More Willing To Help Government Organization	34	22	31	37	38	27	38	36	34	41	30	33	36	32
More Willing To Help Private Organization	34	44	42	31	28	41	34	31	39	30	36	32	33	35
Makes No Difference	19	23	18	17	19	22	16	19	17	18	20	20	17	20
Not Sure	13	11	9	15	15	10	12	14	10	11	14	15	14	13

23

the groups more likely to volunteer—more were willing to work for private organizations than for governmental ones. More people in each of these groups had volunteered their time than those in other socio-economic groups—with more women volunteering than men.

When respondents were asked if they would rather work to help poor people in the United States than to help poor people abroad, 83 per cent answered that they would prefer to help poor Americans, while only 6 per cent stated that they would prefer to help the poor abroad. The greater weight given domestic priorities is even more apparent when the above results are compared with the fact that 68 per cent of the respondents believe the poor of this country to be better off than the poor in other countries. Even 57 per cent of the black population agrees that such is the case. In spite of this awareness, more than four out of five Americans would prefer to work with the poor at home.

In summary, then, while 71 per cent of the public sees hunger and poverty as a very serious world problem deserving of high-priority attention, and while a majority supports increasing domestic poverty allocations, most Americans consider their own personal commitment to solving these problems weak. Although Americans are sympathetic to the problems of the people of the poor countries, they show a definite preference for priority attention to domestic poverty problems for a number of reasons. The findings indicate that Americans consider domestic poverty problems more amenable to solution, and that they see a certain responsibility to tend to national problems before looking elsewhere. Their response also appears to be related to their feeling—discussed in the next chapter—that there is excessive ineffectiveness in the delivery of U.S. foreign assistance to the poor countries.

Other earlier American survey data also indicate that since 1964 Americans have increasingly focused on domestic rather than international problems. Albert Cantril and Charles Roll have reported that in 1971 over three fourths of the public (77 per cent) agreed with the statement: "We shouldn't think so much in *international* terms but concentrate more on our own *national* problems and building up our strength and prosperity at home." In response to the same question asked in 1964 and 1968, only 55 per cent and 60 per cent, respectively, agreed. However, the same authors have also noted that there are "significant differences . . . in the extent to which various population groups favor concentrating on domestic problems. In general, our findings show that the higher the education and income level, the greater the possibility of an internationalist stance."[9] That this concentration on domestic problems is not exclusively American is clear from the large majority of Englishmen who "agreed completely" (65 per cent) or were "inclined to agree" (21 per cent) with the statement: "The government should make sure that the poor people in

---

[9]Albert H. Cantril and Charles W. Roll, Jr., *Hopes and Fears*, pp. 41 and 42.

this country are properly looked after before giving money to other countries."[10]

One can speculate as to the cause of the increasing U.S. preoccupation with domestic concerns. Overwhelming U.S. disillusionment with American involvement in Southeast Asia, urban upheaval, and racial tensions are obviously all contributing factors. Together with the feeling that domestic problems can be solved more easily, affect the average American more directly, and are a more direct U.S. responsibility, these views tilt public concern in favor of domestic issues.

---

[10]I. Rauta, *Aid and Overseas Development*, p. 26.

u.s. foreign assistance

26   Each year Congress invariably engages in the rite of foreign assistance legislation. What the Administration (or Congressional committee) proposes, Congress inevitably disposes—or at least attempts to. Elected officials anxious to establish their credentials as fiscal watchdogs snip away at proposed aid allocations with charges of "Americans are fed up with this drain on the economy," and "enough money down a rathole!" While this perennial exercise is conducted on their behalf, what do Americans in fact think of U.S. foreign assistance? Should the United States provide aid? For what reason? To what ends? How much? What kind? To whom? Through what channels?

In general, the survey responses show that Americans view foreign assistance as primarily a moral or humanitarian responsibility, not as a necessity dictated by international politics; the cold war rationale appears to have lost much of its force with the public. Perhaps the most surprising of the survey's findings is evidence that public support for the concept of U.S. economic assistance to developing countries has not declined, but actually increased considerably over the last decade—although such support is not necessarily translatable into support for increased amounts of assistance. The apparent contradiction between responses offered to the U.S. budget question in the previous chapter and these foreign assistance findings will be discussed at the end of this chapter.

The survey findings also indicate that the U.S. public has a vastly inflated view of the size of the U.S. aid budget compared to the aid programs of other donor nations, and of its actual importance to the poor countries. Conversely, the public—which understands "foreign assistance" only in charitable terms—appears to be almost totally unaware of the positive economic benefits of foreign assistance to the United States, such as its effect on the financing of U.S. exports.

Americans also hold some surprisingly definite preferences for specific types of assistance and channels for its dispensation.

Table III-1. Definitions of "Foreign Aid" (open-ended question)[a]

	Total	Education				Age			
		College Graduates	Some College	High School Graduates	Non-High School Graduates	18-25	26-35	36-50	Over 50
Helping, aiding other countries, people	41%	35%	37%	42%	45%	44%	40%	37%	43%
Sending money to other foreign countries	24	32	28	24	20	30	28	22	19
Sending food to other foreign countries	13	10	14	13	14	12	15	14	10
Handouts, give-aways, wasting money	13	13	13	13	12	5	13	16	15
Providing military assistance to foreign countries to keep world defense up	8	13	11	6	5	12	6	10	3
Helping other countries so they can help themselves	6	7	6	7	5	6	5	7	7

(continued)

Table III-1. (Continued)

	Total	Education				Age			
	Total	College Graduates	Some College	High School Graduates	Non-High School Graduates	18-25	26-35	36-50	Over 50
Providing educational assistance to foreign countries	5%	5%	9%	5%	1%	8%	6%	3%	2%
Sending medical assistance to other foreign countries	4	3	6	3	5	6	4	4	3
Sending supplies to other countries	4	4	3	5	4	2	7	5	3
Giving something for nothing in return	3	3	2	3	3	1	2	4	3
Helping others too much, they should help themselves	3	3	1	3	4	1	1	4	5

[a]Totals do not add up to 100 per cent because respondents could give several answers.

These preferences again reflect the public's overwhelmingly moral and humanitarian justification of U.S. foreign assistance. Americans favor giving those types of assistance which provide the most direct human benefits—such as medical, food, or education assistance. Americans also assign special importance to disaster relief, as well as to educational assistance, which they see as encouraging self-sufficiency—as "helping them to help themselves." Public opinion also appears to favor providing aid to those countries which seem to need it the most.

As for the channels of assistance, Americans are apprehensive about the effectiveness of the U.S. bilateral aid program; they question the efficiency of the U.S. aid bureaucracy and the honesty of some recipient governments and aid bureaucracies. They seem to favor the use of voluntary agency channels—such as the Red Cross and CARE—more than official, government-to-government channels.

WHAT DOES FOREIGN AID MEAN?

The pre-survey focus sessions led us to assume that the phrase "foreign aid" might have negative connotations that we wanted to avoid in the interviews. Throughout the questionnaire, therefore, the words "foreign assistance" were generally used instead—except in those questions which specifically sought to gauge the public's reaction to "aid." In fact, however, the phrase "foreign aid" evoked *positive* reactions from a majority of Americans (58 per cent). Similarly, very few negative connotations were evidenced when respondents were asked, in an open-ended question, what they thought "foreign aid" meant. "Helping other countries and people" by "sending money and food" characterized the responses of more than three quarters (78 per cent) of the respondents. A much smaller group of respondents (19 per cent) considered the words foreign aid to mean "hand-outs, give-aways, wasting money, giving something for nothing in return, helping others too much." Eight per cent more understood foreign aid to mean "providing military assistance to foreign countries to keep world defense up." Older Americans generally were more negative about aid than were younger people. Young Americans as well as Americans of all ages with higher education understood foreign aid to be "financial and military assistance," while those Americans with less education perceived of aid in more general terms, as "helping others."

SUPPORT OR OPPOSITION TO
FOREIGN ASSISTANCE

Respondents were asked to indicate whether they were "strongly in favor, somewhat in favor, somewhat against, or strongly against the United States giving assistance to underdeveloped countries." Better than two thirds of the American public, 68 per cent, are in favor of providing U.S. foreign assistance to the poor countries— with 52 per cent of the public supporting it "somewhat" and 16 per cent "strongly." In contrast, only 28 per cent oppose giving foreign assistance, with 9 per cent of this group opposing it "strongly." In general, relative to other segments of the public, better-educated and younger Americans are more strongly in favor

Table III-2. Support and Opposition to the United States Giving Foreign Assistance

| | In Favor | | | Opposed | | | Not Sure |
	Total	(Strongly)	(Somewhat)	Total	(Strongly)	(Somewhat)	Total
Total	68%	16%	52%	28%	9%	19%	4%
Education							
College Graduates	76	24	52	24	3	21	—
Some College	75	21	54	23	7	16	2
High School Graduates	67	12	55	29	9	20	4
Non-High School Graduates	62	14	48	31	11	20	7
Age							
18-25	74	24	50	21	5	16	5
26-35	69	14	55	28	7	21	3
36-50	67	16	51	28	8	20	5
Over 50	65	12	53	31	13	18	4
Blacks	71	22	49	20	3	17	9

of assistance. Less-educated Americans and older Americans (over fifty years of age) oppose U.S. foreign assistance more strongly than others. Finally, a very small proportion of the public (4 per cent) is "not sure" about its position on U.S. foreign assistance.

A comparison of these results with those of previous surveys reveals an *increase* in support for U.S. foreign assistance from earlier support majorities—from 51 per cent in 1958 and 58 per cent in 1966 to the present level of 68 per cent. It likewise shows a decline in opposition from the previously recorded levels of 31 per cent and 35 per cent to the present level of 28 per cent.[1] Contrary to the widespread assumption that support for foreign assistance is strongly affected by U.S. experience with the Vietnam war, the data suggest that the public position on U.S. foreign assistance in fact has been quite independent of national opinion on Vietnam. At the very time when the war in Southeast Asia was intensifying (1966) and public discontent growing, support for aid increased over the previously recorded high point reached in 1958. In 1972, when our field work was conducted, the end of the Vietnam conflict was in sight, and public support for U.S. foreign assistance reached an historic high of 68 per cent.

What factors have contributed to this increase in support for the idea of giving U.S. foreign assistance? This study demonstrates that there is a close relationship between a respondent's educational level and development sympathy, as well as between his income

31

Figure III-1. **Support and Opposition to the United States Giving Foreign Assitance**[a]

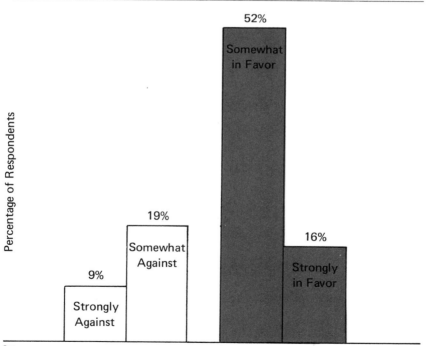

[a]Four per cent of respondents were "not sure."

---

[1]Alfred O. Hero, Jr., "American Public Reactions to Development Assistance." (Study prepared for the Brookings Institution Steering Committee on a possible new organization to develop U.S. public support for aid, Washington, D.C., 1968), p. 58.

Table III-3. Reasons for Helping an Underdeveloped Country (open-ended question)[a]

	Total	Age				Income		
		18-25	26-35	36-50	Over 50	Upper	Middle	Lower
For moral, humanitarian reasons; our responsibility. We should, ought to. They need it. We should help mankind.	29%	30%	29%	30%	29%	38%	28%	27%
To help them help themselves, to make them self-sufficient. To get them on their feet.	18	18	14	20	19	17	19	19
We have so much, have disproportionate share of wealth. Help balance wealthy nations and poor nations.	13	13	11	15	11	13	14	14
To have them as friends, allies; we may need help someday.	10	14	10	9	8	11	10	9
To raise their standard of living, to raise the world's standard of living. To help people have a better life.	8	10	9	6	8	11	7	8

	6%	7%	8%	4%	6%	8%	6%	5%
Would keep down world problems, problems between them and us. Would help to keep the peace, end wars.	6%	7%	8%	4%	6%	8%	6%	5%
Keep them from turning to Communism, keep them free.	6	7	7	6	4	7	6	4
They must be taught, learn new methods. We can teach them technology, industry.	5	3	6	6	6	5	7	4
They have things we want, need—to have access to their natural resources.	5	5	6	6	5	5	7	5
To fight hunger, keep them from starving.	4	4	5	4	4	3	4	5
Would help improve trade, trade relations. Help them increase output to trade on world market.	4	3	3	5	4	5	4	2

[a]Totals do not add up to 100 per cent because respondents could give several answers.

level and development sympathy (see Chapter VI). Americans with higher education and higher incomes are generally more apt to be supporters of development than less-educated, poorer Americans. As the average educational and income levels of American society have risen, so too has support for foreign assistance. As suggested in Chapter II, in the analysis of responses to questions on world conditions and tensions, increased prosperity tends to lift popular development support among all social groupings.

The survey results indicate that a majority of Americans do support giving U.S. economic assistance to underdeveloped countries. It is worth noting that while one out of six Americans is strongly in favor of foreign economic assistance (16 per cent), only one out of eleven (9 per cent) is strongly opposed.

WHY GIVE FOREIGN ASSISTANCE?

The survey shows that Americans favor aid and sympathize with the needs of the developing countries for moral and humanitarian reasons. The U.S. public does not understand development assistance as a *quid pro quo* for securing new supplies of energy or strategic minerals, or for gaining markets in the poor countries. Rather, Americans tend to perceive of U.S. foreign aid as an act of

Table III-4. Reasons for Giving Foreign Assistance (open-ended question)[a]

	Total	Age			
		18-25	26-35	36-50	Over 50
The wealthy should help the poor; people should help each other, we should share, feed hungry people, they need it.	36%	32%	34%	34%	44%
It's our obligation, responsibility, Christian duty, it is our moral duty.	15	10	17	14	18
We should help them enough to help themselves.	13	13	12	13	13
We should help as long as we do not neglect our own.	12	11	14	12	10
We can afford it; we are rich, wealthy. Should be good instead of wasting money on irrelevancies in space.	9	11	11	8	7
Help them in moderation, but don't overdo it. Help them only a little.	7	6	8	7	7
It depends on the kind of assistance. Shouldn't waste money; okay if channeled properly; give goods, not dollars.	7	5	8	7	6
It helps to keep us strong. Keeps them on our side, protects us from Communism.	5	7	1	8	6
It will make a better world, lessen world tensions, will help avoid wars. Poverty breeds violence.	5	6	5	4	4
We should help some countries, but not others.	4	5	4	4	4

[a]Totals do not add up to 100 per cent because respondents could give several answers.

national generosity. Such largesse (in the public's mind) is granted not for political favors, or to prevent the spread of communism, or for mutual benefit, but because it is "right" for the rich to help the poor.

To check again on any negative connotations that the phrase "foreign assistance" might evoke, the questionnaire included separate open-ended questions on the reasons for "favoring foreign assistance" and the reasons for "helping an underdeveloped country." However, the responses offered to the two questions were not markedly different: nearly three quarters of the answers to the first question, and over half of those to the second, were humanitarian or moral. As Table III-4 shows, in answering why the United States should provide foreign assistance, 36 per cent of the American public felt "the wealthy should help the poor; people should help each other; we should share; feed hungry people." An additional 15 per cent said that it was "our obligation, responsibility, Christian duty" to provide foreign assistance to less developed countries.[2] Moreover, in response to another survey question, 82 per cent of those interviewed agreed with the statement that "we help some countries because it is morally right to do so."

Another major reason respondents gave for helping underdeveloped countries and providing foreign assistance was the long-standing rationale of U.S. foreign aid programs that "we should help them help themselves." It is interesting that in answering these open-ended questions, so few respondents suggested deterrence of communism as a reason for helping an underdeveloped country (6 per cent) or for giving foreign assistance (5 per cent). Twenty-six per cent of the responses to these questions expressed certain reservations about the efficacy and purpose of U.S. foreign assistance, as well as about its place among other competing claims on U.S. tax revenue. These objections will be examined in detail later in this chapter.

Much writing and public debate has recently focused on the growing interdependence of nations. Whether this concept is understood by the phrases "spaceship earth" or "global village," in terms of the energy crisis or the growing role of the multinational corporations, the public has been exposed by the media to mounting evidence of growing U.S. economic interdependence with other countries, including underdeveloped countries. Yet in the survey, the American public showed little or no knowledge of these "interdependence issues." While almost 30 per cent of the public believes that the problems faced by the poor in other parts of the world affect the United States a great deal, 36 per cent feels that such problems affect us only somewhat, and 25 per cent believes that the problems of the poor countries do not affect us at all.

---

[2] In the British and Swedish surveys, approximately the same majorities of respondents offered broadly humanitarian or moral reasons for giving aid. See I. Rauta, *Aid and Overseas Development: A Survey of Public Attitudes, Opinions, and Knowledge* (London: Her Majesty's Stationery Office, 1971), p. 28; and Stig Lindholm, *The Image of the Developing Countries: An Inquiry into Swedish Public Opinion* (Uppsala, Sweden: The Dag Hammarskjold Foundation, 1971), p. 56.

Table III-5. Effect of Poverty in Underdeveloped Countries on the United States

	Degree of Effect			
	Great Deal	Somewhat	Hardly Any	Not Sure
Total	30%	36%	25%	9%
Age				
18-25	24	40	30	6
26-35	29	40	20	11
36-50	33	34	24	9
Over 50	30	32	25	13

The same interviewees were then asked the following open-ended question: "In what ways would you say the problems of other people in the world affect us in the United States?" Again, the degree of understanding of this issue correlates closely with the educational background of the respondents. Those Americans with a higher level of formal education appear to believe that the U.S. economy, trade, and political relations, as well as public attitudes, are affected by poor-country problems. People with less education tend to believe that the problems of the poor in other parts of the world affect us less directly: "These problems take money out of our country that could better be used at home; the poor abroad force us to use scarce resources because we are expected to do so." Americans without any college education (roughly two out of three adults) exhibit very little understanding or appreciation of concepts of global interdependence.

Responses to this open-ended question also show that Americans do not view the possibility that poor countries might turn communist as affecting the United States. Thus, although elsewhere in the survey three out of four Americans (71 per cent) agreed with the statement, "If we do not help other countries, the Communists will take them over," the responses to this open-ended question indicate that Americans do not see this prospect as a compelling reason for helping the poor countries. Only a small minority of respondents suggested deterrence of communism as a reason for helping an underdeveloped country or for providing foreign assistance.

Interviewees were presented with two more questions regarding their perceptions of how U.S. aid programs affect developing countries and the United States itself. Responses to these questions indicate that the public has an inflated view of how U.S. aid affects poor countries. This in part might be attributable to the public's misconception of absolute and relative U.S. aid appropriations, as discussed in the previous chapter. Those interviewed were asked: "If the United States decided to stop all of its economic foreign assistance programs, what do you think would happen to the countries we are now helping?" Close to a third of the responses show that interviewees regarded the impact of a suspension of U.S. aid on the poor countries to be minimal. For example, 23 per cent thought the countries would "help them-

Table III-6. Explanations of How Poverty in Underdeveloped Countries Affects the United States (open-ended question)[a]

	Total	Education			
		College Graduates	Some College	High School Graduates	Non-High School Graduates
Takes money out of the country, have to keep sending aid, keeps us from solving our own problems.	15%	8%	11%	18%	19%
Affects us economically.	15	23	15	14	12
Does affect us because we help, we're expected to help; it's our responsibility to help.	12	7	9	12	15
Costs us extra taxes.	11	10	10	13	10
It affects our attitudes, what we think and what we do.	11	13	16	9	9
Affects us militarily, we get involved in their wars.	10	15	7	14	5

(continued)

Table III-6. (Continued)

	Total	Education			
		College Graduates	Some College	High School Graduates	Non-High School Graduates
Affects us politically, causes political issues at home and abroad.	10%	15%	7%	14%	5%
We all have the same problems, their problems are our problems, we are interdependent.	7	12	7	5	5
Affects trade, our trade balance.	5	13	5	4	3
Poverty leads to Communism, they could be exploited by the Communists.	3	3	2	3	2

[a]Totals do not add up to 100 per cent because responses of 2 per cent or less are omitted.

Table III-7. Views on What Would Happen to Countries Now Helped If the United States Stopped All Economic Foreign Assistance Programs (open-ended question)[a]

	Total	Age			
		18-25	26-35	36-50	Over 50
They would help themselves, would learn to rely on themselves, would get along	23%	17%	21%	26%	27%
Communists (China, Russia) would take over; they'd go Communist	20	18	11	9	6
Their growth would stop, they'd go backward back to where they were	16	19	17	16	12
They'd collapse, would go downhill fast, fall apart	13	17	12	9	13
They would get help from someone else, would turn to others for help	11	18	11	9	6
They would starve; hunger	10	9	10	9	11
They would turn on us, would resent us, be anti-American, we would have a lot of enemies	6	8	6	3	6
Some would fall, some would make it on their own	6	4	6	9	5
Reorganization of world power; political upheaval; possible war or revolt	3	3	5	2	3
Other countries would take them over	2	3	2	2	2
Nothing, it wouldn't make much difference one way or another	3	4	4	3	2
All other	2	2	3	2	2
Don't know, not sure	6	5	6	6	8

[a]Totals do not add up to 100 per cent because respondents could give several answers.

selves," and 11 per cent thought they "would get help elsewhere." However, more than half of all responses assumed the effect on underdeveloped countries would be drastic. Twenty per cent predicted communist take-overs; 16 per cent thought growth would stop; 13 per cent thought that the poor countries would collapse; and 10 per cent, that there would be mass starvation.

In response to the open-ended question, "If the United States decided to stop all of its economic foreign assistance programs, what effects do you think it would have on the United States over the long run?," 32 per cent of the respondents thought that U.S. prestige, pride, and popularity would decline. Almost the same percentage of responses indicated that the United States would benefit economically from a cessation of U.S. foreign aid programs. Only one out of every ten respondents thought that U.S. trade (presumably with developing countries) would suffer and import prices would rise as a result of a complete cut-off of aid.

Yet in answer to another question, nearly three quarters of the public (74 per cent) agreed with the statement that "without

Table III-8. Views on What Would Happen to the United States If All U.S. Economic Assistance Programs Were Suspended (open-ended question)[a]

	Total	Age			
		18-25	26-35	36-50	Over 50
Would be less popular, lose friends, allies; would be hated, have more enemies; would hurt relations with other countries	20%	24%	19%	19%	18%
We would have more money to spend at home, more money to fight domestic problems	17	21	19	17	13
Would lose trade, import prices would rise	10	10	9	10	11
Would lose prestige and power, it would weaken national security, hurt us in world opinion	9	10	10	10	7
Nothing, would make no difference, no effect at all	8	8	7	7	8
We would be on our own, isolated, would lead to isolationism	6	8	4	7	4
We would benefit economically	4	4	6	2	4
We would be better off	4	3	4	4	6
Communists would take over, countries would turn to Communism and against the United States	4	4	3	4	5
It might/would cause a war	3	3	3	3	3
Loss of national pride, self-respect, moral commitment	3	2	3	3	3
Taxes would be lower	3	1	3	4	4
Would help stop poverty, create more jobs at home	3	3	4	3	3

[a]Totals do not equal 100 per cent because answers offered by 2 per cent or fewer respondents are omitted.

40

trade with other countries, the United States would suffer considerable economic hardship," and 84 per cent agreed with the statement, "It is really in the best interest of the United States to help poor countries."

Is there a reason behind these apparently contradictory answers? A partial explanation may be in the different types of survey questions that elicited the different responses on U.S.–poor country interdependence. In response to *multiple-choice* questioning, the public consistently chose those answers indicating that American interests are interrelated with those of underdeveloped countries. But when these responses were probed in *open-ended* questions, the public's understanding (especially that of less-educated Americans) of how U.S.–poor country interests are related to one another was shown to be very deficient. The responses merely indicate that Americans do feel that U.S. assistance is in some way also beneficial to the United States. Thus while a large majority of Americans believe that poor-country problems affect the United States, few really know just *how* the United

States is affected or understand how American foreign assistance benefits the United States. This suggests that increased public understanding of how the problems of the poor countries affect the United States and how foreign assistance is in our national self-interest might well increase American interest in, and support for, international development efforts.

PREFERRED FORMS OF ASSISTANCE

Those interviewed tended to consider specific, service-oriented aid as most effective. The public perceives of this type of aid as having benefits that are "immediate, direct, and tangible." All of the kinds of assistance considered *most* effective by the public have these characteristics. On the other hand, financial, trade, and other apparently more abstract assistance forms are viewed as somewhat effective, but less effective than providing medical aid, teachers, books, and tractors. The lack of support for export promotion, freer trade, loans, and financial grants is probably attributable to the lack of understanding that the American public has regarding the importance of such programs to the underdeveloped countries.   41

Table III-9. Views on Effectiveness of Various Forms of Foreign Assistance[a]

	Very Effective	Somewhat Effective	Not Effective
Medical help, doctors, nurses	64%	32%	4%
Teachers, books	61	34	5
Training their students in our universities	58	33	9
Tractors, fertilizers, seed	56	36	8
Aid in birth control	55	31	14
Food, clothing	54	39	7
Send technicians, engineers	52	39	9
Machinery	42	45	13
Spiritual training, missionaries	40	39	21
Help sell their products in U.S.	37	50	13
Provide low interest loans	36	48	16
Lower tariffs, open trade	27	55	18
Investment of U.S. corporations	25	50	25
Financial grants	23	46	31
Military training & equipment	13	37	50

[a]Percentages based on all except "not sure" responses.

Military training and equipment is the type of assistance favored *least* by the American public (49 per cent), with young people most strongly opposed to this type of assistance. Military assistance generally is thought to be ineffective by the largest margin of the public—a response that is strong thoughout this survey as well as consistent with the American response recorded in surveys over the last twenty years.[3] Americans clearly are opposed to military assistance of any kind. Their favorable responses on foreign assistance throughout the survey show that they simply do not think of military assistance when considering foreign aid.

[3]See Alfred O. Hero, Jr., "American Public Reactions . . . ," p. 59, for an analysis of previously recorded attitudes on foreign military assistance.

Table III-10. Type of Foreign Assistance Favored Least[a]

	Total	Age				Income		
		18-25	26-35	36-50	Over 50	Upper	Middle	Lower
Military training and equipment	49%	53%	49%	47%	48%	54%	50%	44%
Financial grants	34	23	37	36	37	32	37	31
Investment of U.S. corporations	21	26	20	20	19	23	20	20
Spiritual training, missionaries	18	34	19	14	9	31	17	9
Low interest loans	13	13	14	11	13	11	15	12
Lower tariffs, open trade	11	12	13	11	10	11	12	11
Help them sell products in U.S.	11	9	13	12	10	12	12	10

[a]Totals do not add up to 100 per cent because respondents could give several answers.

Table III-11. Type of Foreign Assistance Favored Most[a]

	Total	Age				Income		
		18-25	26-35	36-50	Over 50	Upper	Middle	Lower
Medical help, doctors, nurses	52%	54%	51%	48%	54%	53%	52%	51%
Train their students in our universities	29	28	31	32	24	31	32	22
Food, clothing	27	28	27	26	29	24	26	33
Teachers, books	27	33	28	28	20	33	27	21
Aid in birth control	26	29	26	26	22	32	25	21
Tractors, fertilizers, seed	19	20	20	17	20	20	19	21
Technicians, engineers	16	15	20	16	14	20	20	10

[a]Totals do not add up to 100 per cent because respondents could give several answers.

43

There appear to be few differences of opinion among various segments of the public about the types of assistance they consider most effective. Americans overwhelmingly prefer medical assistance for the people of the developing world as a form of foreign aid; 64 per cent considered such assistance very effective. Lower-income Americans are more supportive of food and clothing as essential types of assistance instead of the preference for aid to education shown by the rest of the public. Historically, American public support for both of these types of assistance has been strong.[4]

The major difference of opinion between young and old, rich and poor, concern the effectiveness of missionary activities. For young and upper-income Americans, only military assistance is less popular as a form of assistance. But for lower-income and older (over age fifty) Americans, spiritual training and missionary activity is the form of assistance to which they have the least opposition.

WHICH COUNTRIES SHOULD RECEIVE U.S. ASSISTANCE?

The survey data demonstrate that Americans have some sense of the relative standards of living of developed and developing countries, but have little knowledge of some of the smaller developing countries. Yet the public seems to be aware of those countries, such as Bangladesh, which have suffered unusual disasters in the recent past. There also seems to be a definite public bias for assisting those countries that are the poorest and hence most in need of U.S. assistance.

Respondents were shown a list of seventeen countries and asked a series of questions about them. Some of the questions merely checked on public awareness of these countries, others sought to determine the respondents' knowledge regarding the relative economic standing of these countries; and other questions attempted to elicit the opinion of respondents about giving economic assistance to these countries. Each respondent was asked to

Table III-12. Countries Favored for Receiving U.S. Assistance[a]

	Total	Age			
		18-25	26-35	36-50	Over 50
India	29%	35%	30%	28%	23%
Bangladesh	24	41	22	23	14
Pakistan	13	17	17	11	11
South Korea	12	11	13	12	14
Argentina	10	7	14	9	10
South Africa	10	13	11	9	9
Brazil	10	8	14	10	8

[a]Totals do not add up to 100 per cent because respondents could give several answers.

---

[4]*Ibid.*, p. 60.

identify the two or three countries on the list of seventeen which he favored most for receiving U.S. assistance as well as those which he favored least.

The most highly favored countries for receiving U.S. assistance were India and Bangladesh. Young Americans strongly supported aid to these two countries. This finding contrasts with survey data available from the late 1950s, when aid to "countries like India, which have not joined us as allies against the communists" was not as popular as aid to other poor countries.[5] Such a shift in opinion is probably a function of the diminished role that fear of communism plays today in the American public's view of the world.

In a previous question, Americans had been asked about which two or three of these countries on the list they knew most. The underdeveloped country which respondents felt they knew best was India, which was selected by 24 per cent. The Indian government's rather vigorous public information apparatus in the United States is probably somewhat responsible for such a high recognition factor. Moreover, American youth has shown a special interest in the subcontinent in recent years.

Table III-13. Knowledge About Seventeen Selected Countries[a]

	Total	Education			
		College Graduates	Some College	High School Graduates	Non-High School Graduates
Countries About Which Most Is Known					
Soviet Union	52%	62%	66%	53%	36%
Mainland China	25	27	27	27	18
India	24	30	32	25	16
South Korea	20	14	20	22	21
Egypt	16	21	22	15	11
South Africa	15	16	16	15	13
Brazil	14	20	17	15	8
Argentina	11	18	10	11	9
Pakistan	9	7	11	8	9
Countries About Which Least Is Known					
Tanzania	52	66	61	56	34
Bangladesh	30	31	25	34	26
Kenya	21	24	28	20	16
Bolivia	19	25	25	19	13
Peru	13	12	19	13	10
Mainland China	12	14	16	11	11
Nigeria	12	18	15	10	10
Chile	10	9	12	12	7
Indonesia	9	7	12	10	7

[a]Totals do not add up to 100 per cent because respondents could give several answers.

It is somewhat surprising that a few of the less-developed countries that have been in the news more than others have scored so low on the recognition scale. Bangladesh is a country which Americans rank second on their list of nations most favored for

[5]Alfred O. Hero, Jr., "American Public Reactions . . . ," p. 62.

assistance but also second on the list of countries about which they know least. Americans seem to have a general perception of the magnitude of the problems in Bangladesh from television coverage but probably feel they know little else about this new nation. Tanzania, whose national policies have attracted the attention of a large part of the international development community, nevertheless is the country about which Americans feel they know least. Some anomalies are apparent here, in that certain poor countries that have been in the news in recent years (e.g., Peru, Chile, Nigeria) are not better known by the public. This seems to indicate that only sustained media exposure of particular countries is able to change popular understanding of individual nations.

Table III-14. Ranking of Sixteen Selected Countries by Per Capita Income and GNP[a]

	Per Capita Income	GNP ($ billion)
1. U.S.S.R. (1968)	$1,678	$485.0
2. Argentina (1969)	871	21.0
3. Chile (1969)	675	6.1
4. South Africa (1970)	623	16.0
5. Brazil (1969)	350	32.0
6. Peru (1967)	241	4.0
7. South Korea (1969)	227	7.0
8. Bolivia (1969)	190	.9
9. Kenya (1969)	136	1.4
10. China (1969)	125	80.0
11. Egypt (1968)	102	6.0
12. Pakistan (1965)	89	15.0
13. Indonesia (1970)	80	11.0
14. India (1969)	72	44.0
15. Nigeria (1965)	63	5.0
16. Tanzania (1967)	60	.9

[a]Figures unavailable for Bangladesh.
SOURCE: *New York Times Encyclopedia Almanac* (1971), pp. 651-820.

Despite their generally low level of knowledge regarding the problems and people of the developing world, respondents indicated a surprisingly accurate ability to rank the seventeen countries according to their relative standards of living. Those countries which the public considers to have the highest standard of living are the Soviet Union, Argentina, Brazil, and South Africa. This ranking is in fact accurate, since these four countries are among the five wealthiest from the list of seventeen. Only Chile was omitted, but from the previous question we know that it was ranked as one of the least known countries. India is judged to be the poorest country, followed by Bangladesh, Pakistan, and China.

The responses show a direct relationship between those countries thought to be the least developed and those most favored for U.S. assistance—with the exception of China, which is obviously a special case. Thus while some knowledge about an underdeveloped country is an important ingredient in public support for giving it aid, Americans favor aiding those countries with the greatest demonstrated *need* for assistance.

CHANNELS OF FOREIGN ASSISTANCE

Americans also hold some strong opinions about the inefficiency of the aid bureaucracy and corruption in aid programs. A remarkable 91 per cent of the public (96 per cent of those over age fifty) agree with the statement that "too much of our foreign assistance is kept by the leaders of poor countries and does not get to the people."[6] Eighty-six per cent of the public agrees that "too much foreign aid is wasted in our own bureaucracy and never finds its way abroad"; older Americans are in this instance also more cynical than others. It is interesting that in the British survey, 75 per cent of the British public agreed to a similar statement about its own aid bureaucracy.

Only 27 per cent of Americans (38 per cent of the eighteen to twenty-five year olds) believe that "the United States exploits poor countries just to get what it needs." Englishmen, however, show themselves to be much more skeptical of the intentions of their own government's aid efforts—with 45 per cent agreeing to a similar statement.

Despite the fact that official U.S. government assistance to the poor countries has been declining in recent years, American voluntary aid has been increasing. Given the importance of such voluntary efforts, the survey sought to examine public attitudes on some of the non-governmental programs of foreign assistance. The list of ten organizations on which respondents' views were solicited was not intended to be all-inclusive. Rather, the ten groups were selected because it was thought that the public would be familiar with most of them as well as because of their different approaches to development assistance. Generally, those organizations thought to be helping underdeveloped countries most effectively are also most favored to receive U.S. assistance. Apparently the public considers those organizations with the highest public visibility to be the most effective.

Of the organizations listed, respondents judged the Red Cross, Peace Corps, CARE, and UNICEF to be most effective in helping people in underdeveloped countries. Given the public's demonstrated bias for direct, people-to-people assistance, this finding was hardly surprising. The somewhat lower rankings of the YMCA/YWCA, private foundations, U.S. corporations, and the World Bank was probably not an indication of negative disposition, but a result of the public's unfamiliarity with the overseas work of such organizations. The fact that 25 per cent, 22 per cent, 21 per cent, and 43 per cent of the sample offered "not sure"

---

[6]Sixty-one per cent of the British public responded similarly. See I. Rauta, *Aid and Overseas Development*, p. 41.

Table III-15. Views on Effectiveness of Different Groups Involved in Helping People in Underdeveloped Countries[a]

	Very Effective	Somewhat Effective	Not Effective	Not Sure
Red Cross	51%	33%	10%	6%
Peace Corps	50	38	6	6
CARE	50	37	5	8
UNICEF	38	34	7	21
Religious Groups	33	48	13	6
United Nations	29	43	17	11
YMCA/YWCA	18	39	18	25
Private Foundations	17	46	15	22
U.S. Corporations	15	45	19	21
World Bank	11	30	16	43

[a]Totals do not add up to 100 per cent because respondents could give several answers.

answers, respectively, on the four organizations mentioned, provides further evidence of general public ignorance of their activities.

Respondents were then asked which two or three organizations should receive the largest shares if the U.S. government were to decide to give more of its foreign assistance money to organizations like those on the list rather than directly to countries. Under-

Table III-16. Views on Giving Foreign Assistance to Organizations or Directly to Countries

	Total	Age			
		18-25	26-35	36-50	Over 50
Give to Organizations	57%	64%	59%	57%	49%
Give to Countries	22	22	23	21	23
Not Sure	21	14	18	22	28

standably, those organizations thought to be most effective were most favored to receive U.S. assistance. The Peace Corps—whose budget allocation in fact has been cut recently—was most strongly supported by 57 per cent of all respondents and by 90 per cent of those between the ages of eighteen and twenty-five. While 28 per cent of those interviewed said in response to this question that they would favor increasing support to UNICEF, only 13 per cent said they would favor giving more to the United Nations. CARE and the Red Cross were both supported by 46 per cent of the sample, and religious groups by 29 per cent. The four organizations that rank last on the priority list maintained that position probably for the same reason of low recognition.

This study originally intended to gauge American opinion on questions of bilateral versus multilateral assistance—despite the relatively low public comprehension of this issue. No survey questions dealt directly with the multilateral versus bilateral aid debate, however, since the pre-survey focus sessions indicated that questions on this subject have no meaning for Americans. Alfred Hero observed in 1968 that "majorities of minorities who have *heard* of UNESCO, refugee and relief activities of U.N. agencies . . . have approved of U.S. participation in them, including their financial support. However, suggestions that much U.S. capital aid or that most, or considerably more, of even its technical assistance be channeled through the U.N. system . . . were favorably received by only minorities of the American public during the 1950s."[7]

Since only a small minority could be expected to have any knowledge of the distinction between bilateral and multilateral assistance, the following, less specific question was asked instead in the survey: "It has been suggested that the United States government should give more of its foreign assistance money to organizations like the ones on this list and give less money directly to the countries. Do you feel that the U.S. government should give to organizations or should it give the money to the governments of the countries themselves?" It must be cautioned, however, that the strong (57 per cent) bias to give money to organizations as distinct from governments (22 per cent) is not necessarily equatable with support for shifting bilateral aid programs to multilateral channels. Instead, it is more likely that these responses reflect public suspicion of inefficiency and ineffectiveness in government aid programs, as well as a more general suspicion of all government programs.

CONCLUSION

Public skepticism about the efficiency of government programs versus privately funded programs also seems to be behind two inconsistencies that emerged in the survey responses. As we saw earlier, 68 per cent of all Americans favor the idea of giving U.S. foreign economic assistance, yet 43 per cent favor budget cuts in U.S. assistance. And a majority of 57 per cent of Americans agree while only 31 per cent disagree that "foreign aid should come from voluntary contributions rather than taxes." How can more Americans than ever before favor giving economic assistance, yet at the same time want to cut the U.S. foreign aid budget, and want aid to come from voluntary contributions rather than taxes? Part of the explanation is likely to be the low regard the public has for government aid programs (which it considers inefficient) relative to voluntary aid efforts (which it considers more efficient). It is important to note that all previous U.S. and European survey data on foreign assistance reflect similar inconsistencies. The public has never been completely logical on issues of international poverty and development. Moreover, it is also significant that while 43

---

[7] Alfred O. Hero, Jr., "American Public Reactions . . . ," p. 64. Italics added.

per cent seeks cuts in economic assistance, 49 per cent favors either maintaining (41 per cent) or increasing (8 per cent) the aid budget.

Perhaps more important, the budget question responses should be considered in light of the data on the public's conception of both the actual size of the U.S. aid allocations, and their relative size compared to those of other developed countries. As reported in the last chapter, 75 per cent of the American public believes the U.S. aid budget should—in terms of the share of wealth devoted to development assistance—be greater than (20 per cent) or equal to (55 per cent) those of other developed countries. In fact, only 2 per cent of the public knows that, in these terms, the U.S. aid effort today is indeed relatively much smaller than those of other rich nations. Equally few Americans are fully aware of the stark dimension of poverty in the developing countries and the absolute misery in which a majority of the world's population lives. The final chapter of this monograph will demonstrate that as Americans become more aware of the magnitude of global poverty problems, and of the standing of the United States among other donor nations, their opinions are likely to shift in favor of greater U.S. support for development efforts.

international trade

There is little dispute among development specialists that more   51
liberal and equitable trade policies on the part of the industrialized
world toward the products of the developing countries would give
a powerful boost to development. Trade now provides more than
two thirds of the foreign exchange earnings of the developing
world. Approximately 80 per cent of the total financial flows
from rich to poor nations is accounted for by trade; aid and private investment together amount to only 20 per cent of the total.

U.S. trade with the poor countries is also of real benefit to
the American economy and consumers. In 1972 the United States
exported $16.3 billion of goods to developing countries (only $0.5
billion less than total exports to the enlarged European Economic
Community and Japan), and imported $15.3 billion of commodi-
ties and manufactures from poor countries. While the United
States sustained almost a $5 billion deficit in its trade balance with
the European Economic Community and Japan, trade with the
poor countries was $1 billion in *surplus.* Because of this impor-
tance of trade to poor countries and the United States alike, as
well as the current national debate on U.S. trade policy, the survey
sought to determine American opinions on a number of questions
concerning trade with the developing countries.

Surprisingly, the findings show that the sizable portion of the
public (41 per cent) that supports freer trade with the poor countries in principle does so largely because it regards liberal U.S.
trade policies as an important form of assistance to the poor countries. The survey data show that the numbers of these liberal trade
supporters would grow considerably (to 67 per cent) if it were
certain that American workers whose jobs were adversely affected
by increased imports would be provided with adequate adjustment
assistance. Those who tend to favor freer trade with developing
countries are generally college-educated, in the upper-income
bracket, and politically "liberal." However, it is interesting that
the responses show no discernible differences in opinion on trade
questions between union and non-union workers; union workers

Table IV-1. Attitudes Toward Import Restrictions

	On Goods From Wealthy Countries			On Goods From Underdeveloped Countries		
	Approve 72%	Disapprove 15%	Not Sure 12%	Approve 44%	Disapprove 39%	Not Sure 16%
Total						
Education						
College Graduates	77	18	5	44	50	6
Some College	75	18	7	35	55	10
High School Graduates	74	15	11	54	33	13
Non-High School Graduates	65	14	20	40	33	27
Occupation						
Professional/Executive	81	13	6	48	46	6
White Collar	79	16	5	52	41	8
Blue Collar	71	16	13	43	39	18
Age						
18-25	73	16	10	36	52	12
26-35	78	14	9	52	38	10
36-50	74	15	11	47	38	15
Over 50	65	19	17	41	34	24
Income						
Upper	80	14	7	48	46	7
Middle	78	15	7	47	42	12
Lower	60	17	23	40	32	28

are not more strongly opposed to freer trade than are non-union workers.

The survey results also indicate that while the U.S. public generally looks favorably on U.S. foreign investment in the poor countries as a moderately effective form of foreign assistance, Americans overwhelmingly reject the idea of government compensation for corporations whose property is expropriated by foreign governments.

REASONS FOR SUPPORTING AND OPPOSING FREE TRADE

In answer to a series of our survey questions on U.S. trade policy, nearly three out of four respondents (72 per cent) approved of import restrictions on goods from wealthy countries such as West Germany and Japan, but only 44 per cent similarly approved of restrictions on imports from developing countries. While college graduates, upper-income respondents, and professionals were more protectionist concerning U.S. trade policy toward other industrialized nations, they were characteristically more favorably disposed than other groups to liberal trade with the poor countries. These responses indicate that Americans make important distinctions between rich and poor trading partners.

Those interviewed were shown a card listing four basic arguments favoring free trade with the underdeveloped nations. After respondents had reviewed these, they were asked to identify the most important reason for favoring free trade. Contrary to expectations, respondents did not select "lower prices for the American consumer by allowing in lower-priced goods from other countries" as the most compelling reason in support of free trade. Instead, 40 per cent of the respondents—more than twice as many as selected any other reason—considered the most important reason for favoring free trade to be the fact that such a policy is an inducement to the development of the poor countries.

Respondents were also asked to study a card listing four basic reasons against free trade. Half of the respondents (49 per cent) judged the displacement of American workers the most important reason to oppose free trade. This concern about the impact of free trade on domestic employment was shared by Americans of all backgrounds—with those in the upper-income category indicating a higher degree of concern than those in the lower-income group.

These initial opinions expressed by respondents were then probed further with the question: "Now that you have read some of the arguments about free trade with underdeveloped countries, would you say you basically favor the idea of free trade, or oppose it?" While only 2 per cent more respondents now favored free trade, 10 per cent fewer respondents opposed such a policy, and 9 per cent more were now "not sure." Table IV-4 displays the percentage spreads of those who opposed freer trade with underdeveloped countries (i.e., favored import restrictions) or were not sure *before* reading the arguments, and the same spread of respondents who opposed or were not sure *after* reading the arguments.

Table IV-2. Reasons for Favoring Free Trade with Underdeveloped Countries

Reasons	Total	Education				Age			
		College Graduates	Some College	High School Graduates	Non-High School Graduates	18-25	26-35	36-50	Over 50
Free trade is good for the United States to assist the economic development of under-developed countries.	40%	44%	47%	39%	33%	44%	42%	39%	36%
Free trade would stimulate international competition and would open new markets for U.S. products.	18	27	22	18	13	15	19	22	16
Free trade would lower prices for the American consumer by allowing in lower-priced goods from other countries.	14	12	15	14	15	18	15	11	14
Free trade would result in increased American exports and thus would create more jobs in our export industries.	9	7	8	10	11	10	8	9	11
Not Sure	19	10	8	19	28	13	16	19	23

Table IV-3. Reasons for Opposing Free Trade with Underdeveloped Countries

Reasons	Total	Type of Occupation			Income		
		Professional/Executive	White Collar	Blue Collar	Upper	Middle	Lower
Free trade would put some American laborers out of work because their jobs can be done by foreign labor at much lower cost.	49%	47%	47%	52%	53%	50%	44%
Free trade would force some American businessmen into unfair competition because of the lower production costs in other countries.	14	16	21	13	17	15	12
Free trade would intensify the problem the United States now faces in maintaining a favorable trade balance.	14	19	16	11	15	15	12
Free trade would make the United States too dependent upon other countries for essential goods.	5	5	8	4	5	6	5
Not Sure	18	13	8	20	10	14	27

55

Table IV-4. Opposition to Free Trade with Underdeveloped Countries Before and After Reading the Arguments

| | Before | | After | |
	In favor of import restrictions	Not sure	Opposed to free trade	Not sure
Total	44%	16%	34%	25%
Education				
College Graduates	44	6	33	14
Some College	35	10	32	15
High School Graduates	54	13	38	26
Non-High School Graduates	40	27	32	35
Occupation				
Professional/Executive	48	6	34	15
White Collar	52	8	42	19
Blue Collar	43	18	31	28
Age				
18-25	36	12	32	19
26-35	52	10	38	22
36-50	47	15	33	29
Over 50	41	24	35	28

The survey indicates that a considerable percentage of those who initially opposed free trade (10 per cent) were willing to reconsider their position after brief exposure to the basic trade debate arguments. This suggests a considerable potential role for public education on this range of issues.

VIEWS ON ADJUSTMENT ASSISTANCE

To explore further the depth and nature of opposition to freer trade, the 34 per cent of respondents who continued to oppose free trade even after considering the arguments, and the 25 per cent who were not sure, were then asked: "If American workers who lost their jobs because of free trade did not suffer any personal financial loss and were retrained in jobs equal to or better than their old ones, would you basically favor the idea of free trade, or oppose it?" Since "worker displacement" was assumed to be the major negative factor weighed by respondents in their consideration of freer trade, this question sought to find out public opinion on remedial action—adjustment assistance—to counter this factor.

When asked to assume adequate worker compensation and retraining, over half of the respondents who previously opposed free trade said they would favor such a policy, and about one fourth of those who were initially unsure said they would shift to favor free trade. Thus we found that free trade would be favored by two out of three Americans (67 per cent), and would be opposed by only 15 per cent, if the conditions of worker compensation and retraining were met.

Surprisingly, responses to the entire series of questions on trade indicate that union households in this country are no more, and maybe even somewhat less, protectionist than non-union households. Union households, like non-union households, were initially somewhat more against than for free trade. However, when asked to assume an adequate adjustment assistance provi-

Table IV-5. Attitudes Toward Free Trade With and Without Adjustment Assistance Condition

	Without Adjustment Assistance	With Adjustment Assistance
Favor	41%	67%
Oppose	34	15
Not Sure	25	18

sion, more union households which initially opposed liberalizing U.S. trade policy with the developing countries switched to favoring such a policy than did non-union households. Thus it seems that if an adequate adjustment assistance program were developed, the already strong sentiment for liberal trading policies could be considerably increased. Such findings cast real doubt on assumptions regarding the public's alleged protectionist persuasion.[1]

Table IV-6. Comparison of Union and Non-Union Attitudes Toward Free Trade With and Without Adjustment Assistance Condition

	Union		Non-Union	
	Without Adjustment Assistance	With Adjustment Assistance	Without Adjustment Assistance	With Adjustment Assistance
Favor	40%	51%	39%	42%
Oppose	46	21	45	28

FOREIGN INVESTMENT

Though foreign investment was not a major subject of inquiry in this survey, respondents' opinions were sought on two statements regarding U.S. private investment overseas. Fifty-five per cent of the public agreed that "our government should do more to encourage businessmen to invest in underdeveloped countries," and 32 per cent disagreed. Yet when asked whether "the United States should pay back the money corporations lose when they are nationalized by other countries," only 13 per cent concurred, while 64 per cent disagreed. Thus the public quite definitely opposes using tax revenue for compensating expropriated companies.

In answer to two other questions on the activities of overseas private corporations, approximately three out of five respondents said they regarded U.S. foreign investment as a "somewhat" or "very effective" way of assisting the development of the poor countries with about one out of five labeling such assistance "not effective."

---

[1] For an interesting discussion of the attitudes of European manual workers on trade issues see Ruth Padrun, "Attitudes and Motivations of Manual Workers in Industry Concerning Development Issues," Report of an International Pilot Study prepared for Action for Development, of the U.N. Food and Agriculture Organization (Paris: International Institute of Research and Training in Education and Development, August 1972).

youth and development

58 Seldom has one generation been alternately as maligned and extolled, imitated and ridiculed, as American youth has been over the past decade. Most recently, young Americans have been labeled neo-isolationist and judged cynical, spent, apathetic. They are supposedly "turned off" to seeking social change and world peace and "turned on" to personal fulfillment.

The results of the survey[1] show that the twenty-nine million Americans between the ages of eighteen and twenty-five are generally more sympathetic to social issues—development among them—and less concerned with questions of national defense and military security than their elders. They favor increasing, or at least maintaining, present spending levels on all social welfare programs; and they assign top priority to the solution of world hunger and poverty.

Young people generally, and college youth in particular, are more liberal, less religious, and better informed on development issues than are adults. Much of the liberal hue of the views of this age group is determined by the high percentage of college students that it includes. More than one third (34 per cent) of all eighteen to twenty-five year olds are presently enrolled in colleges, and another 23 per cent have attended college (19 per cent of this 23 per cent being four-year graduates, and 6 per cent postgraduates). Yet college experience alone does not explain this age group's liberal orientation on domestic and international social issues, since its non-college members also exhibit more liberal attitudes than their elders. Whether this is so because the general quality of formal and informal education has improved, or because of a marked change in the socialization process, is a subject for other analyses to explore.

---

[1]This survey of attitudes of young people between the ages of eighteen and twenty-five results from a separate but parallel survey sponsored by the U.S. Coalition for Development. The same basic questionnaire was used in both surveys.

POVERTY AND DEVELOPMENT

Young Americans regard global development problems as more serious than do adults, and also accord these problems higher priority attention than adults. While the disparity in opinion is most pronounced between adults and college youth, a marked difference also exists between youth as a whole and adults. More than four out of five young Americans (81 per cent) consider hunger and poverty a very serious world problem, while only 68 per cent of Americans twenty-six years of age and older agree with such an assessment. An overwhelming 86 per cent of American college students see world hunger and poverty as a very serious problem, as do 80 per cent of their non-college peers. Moreover, 44 per cent of all youth consider this problem worthy of "top priority" attention.

Table V-1. Comparison of Youth and Adult Views on Relative Seriousness of World Problems[a]

World Problem	Very Serious		Top Priority	
	Youth	Adult	Youth	Adult
Hunger and Poverty	81%	68%	44%	41%
Pollution	75	63	35	22
Using Up Natural Resources	75	64	26	16
Overpopulation	67	51	27	14
Drug Abuse	67	83	32	49
Hatred Between Racial and Ethnic Groups	63	56	20	16
Corrupt Government	62	58	22	23
Lack of Communication Among People	60	54	15	13
Poor Medical Care	59	49	14	18
Communism	49	63	13	22
Lack of Adequate Housing	48	39	6	7

[a]Percentages based on those respondents who had already identified the issues as problems.

Three out of four young Americans (75 per cent) regard problems of pollution and the depletion of natural resources as "very serious" world problems; 35 per cent and 26 per cent give these problems, respectively, top priority attention. Overpopulation is thought to be the next most serious world problem by more than two thirds (67 per cent) of American youth; 27 per cent rate it as a problem deserving top priority attention.

In comparison, the adult response to these problems is considerably weaker. Only 63 per cent consider problems of pollution "very serious," and only 64 per cent are seriously worried about the depletion of natural resources. Considerable differences between youth and adult reactions are also evident in the priority ranking given these problems by the two groups. Twenty-two per cent of all adults—compared to 35 per cent of youth—place pollution problems in the "top priority" category; and only 16 per cent of adults give "top priority" ranking to the problems of using up natural resources. Adults also appear to be less concerned with overpopulation; only 51 per cent, compared to 67 per cent of youth, regard it as "very serious."

Two problems of great concern to adults—drug abuse (83 per cent) and communism (63 per cent)—are much less worrisome to young Americans (67 per cent and 49 per cent, respectively). Whereas adults place communism fourth in priority for attention as a world problem, young people rank it tenth.

Some dramatic differences of opinion are also evident between college and non-college youth. Notably, 52 per cent of student youth consider drug abuse a very serious world problem compared to 78 per cent of non-college youth. Other, less striking differences of opinion between these two groups are also evident on problems of the depletion of natural resources, which 80 per cent of college youth and 69 per cent of non-college youth consider a very serious problem, and on problems of overpopulation, which 75 per cent of college youth and 61 per cent of non-college youth see as very serious.

Table V-2. Comparison of College and Non-College Youth Ranking of "Very Serious" World Problems[a]

World Problem	Total	Percentage Ranking Problem "Very Serious"	
		Non-College	In College
Hunger and Poverty	81%	80%	86%
Pollution	75	74	77
Using Up Natural Resources	75	69	80
Overpopulation	67	61	75
Drug Abuse	67	78	52
Hatred Between Racial and Ethnic Groups	63	61	66
Corrupt Government	62	60	64
Lack of Communication Among People	60	52	65
Poor Medical Care	59	59	60

[a]Percentages based on those respondents who had already identified the issues as problems.

Although youth and adult respondents generally agree that lack of education is a basic factor in explaining why people are poor, there are striking dissimilarities between generations in other responses to the question of why people are poor. Fewer than one third of young Americans—30 per cent of all those eighteen to twenty-five years of age and only 23 per cent of college youth— consider "laziness" a determining factor, compared to the 43 per cent of adults who express this view.

Young Americans generally, and college students in particular, offered reasons such as "they are born into it," "the only life

Table V-3. Comparison of Youth and Adult Views on Why Poor People Are Poor (open-ended question)[a]

	Total Youth	Non-College	In College	Adult
Lack of education, ignorance, illiteracy	42%	44%	41%	43%
Lazy, no ambition, no drive, don't get out and work, want to be poor, prefer welfare	30	33	23	43
Lack of opportunity, never had a chance, can't get decent jobs, don't have equal opportunity	29	30	30	24
They are born into it, the only life they know, it's environmental, they inherit it	25	17	35	18
They are victims of the system, the social structure, government	10	6	18	5
Not enough job training, no skills	5	6	4	4
Some are just less fortunate, in the wrong place at the wrong time	3	2	4	3
Rich people keep them down, won't help	3	3	4	2
Overpopulation, large families, too many children	3	3	3	2
Handicapped, poor health, illness	3	3	3	7

[a]Totals do not add up to 100 per cent because respondents could give several answers.

they know," "it's environmental," or "they inherit it" to explain poverty much more frequently than did adults in response to the question of why people are poor. In contrast to the 25 per cent of young Americans who gave these reasons, only 18 per cent of adult Americans offered similar responses. Adults and youth agree however, on the "lack of equal opportunity" or a "decent chance" as a cause of poverty. Yet, while almost one out of five college students believes that poor people are the "victims of the system, the social structure, the government," only one out of twenty adults faults the system with determining why people are poor. A majority of the responses that youth offered to this question blamed poverty on factors beyond the control of poor people— that is, "lack of opportunity, they are born into it, they are victims of the system." About one of every three adult responses expressed this view compared to half of all college youth answers.

U.S. BUDGET PRIORITIES

The survey results show that a majority of youth would increase or at least maintain present spending levels on every social welfare budget item while cutting all military expenditures. College youth overwhelmingly favor such action. While only 5 per cent of American adults favor *increasing* the budgetary allocations for foreign

Table V-4. Comparison of Youth, Adult, and General Population Views
on Allocation of U.S. Budget

	Total Youth	Non-College	In College	Adults	General Population
Budget Items Respondents Felt Should Be Increased[a]					
Education	83%	77%	87%	64%	68%
Pollution Control	81	73	92	61	65
Medical Services	59	57	64	49	51
Social Security	49	54	44	51	50
Economic Assistance to Foreign Countries	20	14	29	5	8
Budget Items Respondents Felt Should Be Kept the Same[a]					
Food Stamps	38	38	35	41	40
Economic Assistance to Foreign Countries	45	45	44	41	41
Farm Price Supports	38	37	38	38	38
National Defense	36	43	24	48	46
Military Assistance to Foreign Countries	37	39	38	38	38
Budget Items Respondents Felt Should Be Decreased[a]					
Military Assistance to Foreign Countries	53	47	58	51	52
National Defense	54	40	73	35	38
Space Research	35	42	29	46	44
Economic Assistance to Foreign Countries	29	32	24	47	43

[a]Totals do not add up to 100 per cent because respondents could give several answers.

economic assistance, 20 per cent of eighteen to twenty-five year olds as a whole, and 29 per cent of all college youth favor such an increase. At the other extreme, 47 per cent of adults would opt for *decreasing* economic assistance, compared to 29 per cent of youth generally, and 24 per cent of college youth.

The difference between youth and adult opinion is most striking on the question of allocations for "national defense." While almost three out of four (73 per cent) college students would cut national defense expenditures, only 35 per cent of adults would do likewise—a disparity of 38 per cent. Youth and adults agree, however, that military aid should be decreased. Thus the budgetary priorities of young people are quite clear: they would increase spending on major domestic social programs and decrease military expenditures. While adults are divided on the question of foreign economic assistance allocations—5 per cent would increase, 41 per cent maintain, and 47 per cent cut them— nearly two thirds (65 per cent) of all young Americans would either increase or maintain present levels of economic assistance.

PERSONAL COMMITMENT

We have seen that young Americans consider world development problems as very serious and worthy of top priority attention, but how do they view their own personal level of commitment to solving these problems? Only 15 per cent consider their commitment "very strong." A much larger group, 43 per cent, rank their commitment as "fairly strong," and 39 per cent of all young Americans characterize it as "not strong." Adults evaluate their own commitment level less severely—with 22 per cent judging their commitment "very strong," 42 per cent "fairly strong," and 30 per cent "not strong."

These responses were fairly constant for nearly every subgroup of younger people questioned. Differences in perception of commitment level between income groups, between college and non-college youth, and between those who have and have not helped as volunteers on poverty projects, were virtually nonexistent. More of those young people (49 per cent) who had visited developing countries felt that their commitment was "not strong" than those who had not (39 per cent); the first-hand confrontation of the effects of underdevelopment probably makes for more severe judgment of the extent of one's involvement.

In response to a further question about personal commitment, 28 per cent of all eighteen to twenty-five year olds stated that they were doing "as much as can be expected" to solve problems of hunger and poverty, 44 per cent offered that they were doing "less than expected" (56 per cent of college youth), 20 per cent said they were doing "nothing at all," and only 5 per cent (10 per cent of college youth) credited themselves with "doing all they can."

63

FOREIGN ASSISTANCE

As already noted in the earlier chapter on foreign assistance, our survey results indicate that public support levels for the concept of assistance to the poor countries has risen by some 17 per cent since surveys conducted in 1958 and 1966. These earlier surveys of public positions on foreign aid showed that younger Americans (twenty to twenty-nine years of age) generally have supported economic assistance to a greater degree than their elders. In this survey, we found that although the contrast in aid support is somewhat reduced if different age groups of similar educational background are compared, young Americans nevertheless tend to be considerably more supportive of aid than adults. Thus while even non-college youth favor aid more than their elders, the opinion cleavage is most striking between college students and adults. An overwhelming four out of five (81 per cent) college students favor the idea of U.S. foreign assistance compared to 68 per cent of non-college and 67 per cent of adults.

Further contrast between adults and younger people is evident from the percentages in each group that "strongly" favor U.S. foreign assistance. Twenty-four per cent of all youth, and 30

Table V-5. Comparison of Youth and Adult Views on Foreign Assistance

	Total Youth	Non-College	In College	Adult
Strongly In Favor	24%	20%	30%	14%
Somewhat In Favor	50	48	51	53
Somewhat Against	16	19	14	20
Strongly Against	5	6	3	9
Not Sure	5	7	2	4

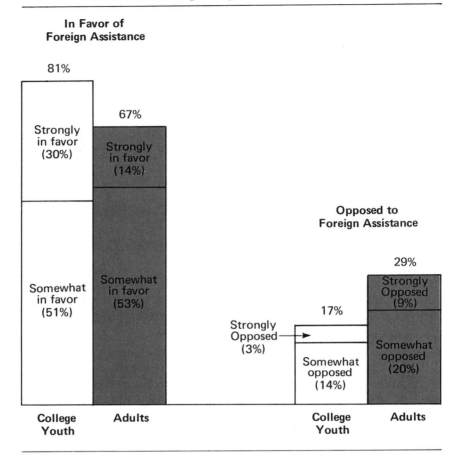

Figure V-1. Comparison of College Youth and Adult Views on the United States Giving Foreign Assistance

In Favor of Foreign Assistance

81%

Strongly in favor (30%)

67%

Strongly in favor (14%)

Somewhat in favor (51%)

Somewhat in favor (53%)

Opposed to Foreign Assistance

29%

Strongly Opposed (9%)

17%

Strongly Opposed (3%)

Somewhat opposed (14%)

Somewhat opposed (20%)

College Youth   Adults   College Youth   Adults

per cent of college youth, strongly favor U.S. foreign assistance—compared to 14 per cent of the adult population. The contrast between youth and adult opinion is also apparent in a comparison of the percentages of foreign assistance opponents. Twenty-nine per cent of adult Americans, but only 17 per cent of college youth, oppose the concept of U.S. foreign assistance.

REASONS FOR DEVELOPMENT SUPPORT

When American perceptions of U.S. interdependence with other countries—including developing countries—were examined earlier in Chapter III, it was concluded that the public had no clear conception of how U.S. national interests and the development of the poor countries were interrelated. While this finding was also true of youth opinion, college students frequently stated that the problems of poor people from other countries do affect American attitudes and, in some vague sense, American behavior. But this slightly more sophisticated comprehension of the national self-interest rationale for global development is not strong enough to account for the considerably more favorable orientation of young people to development concerns. Both youth and adult development support is clearly predicated on humanitarian and moral concerns.

While young people evidence no greater understanding of interdependence issues than do adults, they nevertheless are more

Table V-6. How Problems of Poor in Other Parts of the World Affect the United States (open-end question)[a]

	Total Youth	Non-College	In College	Adults
Affect us economically	15%	12%	19%	16%
Affect our attitudes, what we think and what we do	15	10	23	10
We are expected to help, it is our responsibility to help	13	17	7	11
Take money out of the country, have to keep sending aid	12	16	9	16
Affect us militarily, get involved in their wars	9	9	8	10
We all have the same problems, their problems are our problems	9	6	12	6
Cost us extra taxes	9	9	6	12
Affect trade, our trade balance	5	3	8	6
Affect us politically, cause political issues	5	2	9	3

[a]Responses of 2 per cent or less are omitted.

informed on these issues than any other age group. This, however, is undoubtedly a result of the higher educational level of this group compared to other generations.

OTHER CHARACTERISTICS OF YOUTH OPINION

Despite some of these striking differences in opinion between young adults and their elders, one half of all young Americans consider their attitudes to be either "almost" or "somewhat" the same as those of their parents. Another 48 per cent, however, regard their attitudes as "fairly" or "completely" different from those of their parents. Expectedly, non-college youth feel more closely aligned to their parents' attitudes than do their college peers. Similarly, youth-adult opinion cleavages are more dramatic between college youth and adults than they are between youth as a whole and adults.

In ideology, 42 per cent of all youth (59 per cent of college youth) regard themselves as "left of moderate." Another 34 per cent consider themselves "moderate" (25 per cent of college youth) and 16 per cent of all young Americans perceive themselves "right of moderate" (14 per cent of college youth). Fifteen per cent of young Americans in college consider themselves as "far left" (13 per cent) or "radical left" (2 per cent), while only 5 per cent of their non-college peers describe themselves as "far" or "radical" left. Of the 71 per cent of young people who were registered to vote (55 per cent non-college, 85 per cent college youth), 45 per cent listed Democrat, 21 per cent Republican, and 27 per cent (31 per cent of college students) Independent.

While more than half (56 per cent) of American adults consider religion to have influenced their lives "strongly" or a "great deal," only 38 per cent of American youth makes this assertion. Others indicate that religion has influenced their lives "somewhat" (35 per cent) or "hardly at all" (25 per cent), compared to the 30 per cent and 13 per cent of adults who feel this way.

Thus our findings show that Americans between the ages of eighteen and twenty-five years are the most easily identifiable segment of the public showing a strong sympathy for development. Clearly part of the explanation for this sympathetic orientation is the high educational attainment of young Americans. (The correlation of development sympathy with education will be discussed further in the next chapter.)

But what determines the favorable development orientation of non-college youth? Has American primary and secondary education improved in recent years? Are there more and better channels of "informal" education available to today's youth? Have the electronic media played some role in forming youth's attitudes about the world? Although these questions are interesting, they go beyond the survey data available for this study. While the data cannot determine the "reasons" for youth's favorable position on development issues, they do suggest that any attempt to increase U.S. development support would ignore young Americans only at its own expense.

development information
and sympathy:
a national overview

Our analysis of responses in previous chapters shows that there is a certain degree of ambivalence and inconsistency in American attitudes on a variety of development issues. We have seen, for example, that while 68 per cent of the American public favors giving U.S. foreign assistance to underdeveloped countries, 43 per cent wants to cut the amount of economic assistance in the federal budget. Similar apparent contradictions emerge from other parts of the survey results. Obviously, then, no one question can provide a very accurate indication of American opinion on global poverty and development issues.

To gain a better understanding of the public's support for development needs, and to establish some standard by which to judge the various attitudes expressed in the survey, indices were constructed to measure how well informed and how sympathetic the public is on development problems and issues. These indices were then used in preparing profiles of those Americans who are sympathetic or unsympathetic about international development and to identify some distinguishing characteristics of those Americans informed or uninformed about development issues.

THE SYMPATHY INDEX

The sympathy index consists of the nine survey questions considered to be the best measure of personal commitment to, and public support for, international development efforts. An individual who is "sympathetic" considers global development problems to be very serious and deserving of top priority attention. A sympathetic respondent also approves of vigorous government action to alleviate poverty at home as well as abroad and is likely to be personally committed to helping solve such problems. Conversely, an "unsympathetic" respondent opposes government expenditures on international poverty programs and is likely to consider the national commitment to global development efforts overextended and unimportant. The views of the "uncommitted" group of respondents lie somewhere between the extremes of sympathy and the lack of it. A complete description of this index and a listing of the questions comprising it can be found in Annex D.

THE INFORMATION INDEX

This survey was not conducted for the primary purpose of determining how much Americans know about the precise facts and figures of development simply because previous surveys have demonstrated, over the years, that very few Americans score high on information questions regarding the foreign assistance program. This being the case, the survey did not repeat objective questions of that nature. Nevertheless, a number of questions did provide us with some indication of how well informed the public is on several basic development issues. We therefore were able to assess public awareness on a few of the issues on which one would expect a well informed public to score high (such as the relative percentage of people living in the developing world, or the relative economic ranking of certain developed and developing countries). Since the information index is not intended to be a precise mechanism for determining the knowledge of respondents, only the responses of those at each extreme of the index—those judged to be very well informed or uninformed—were analyzed. A detailed analysis of this index also can be found in Annex D.

PROFILES OF THE "SYMPATHETIC"
AND THE "INFORMED"

Two out of every five (38 per cent) Americans can be regarded as basically sympathetic to the concerns and needs of the developing world and therefore potential supporters of a vigorous U.S. response to such needs. At the other end of the opinion spectrum, 25 per cent of Americans are negatively disposed toward the needs and interests of the poor countries. A large balance, 37 per cent, can be characterized as uncommitted. They are neither positively nor negatively predisposed on most development issues but are likely to shift on any specific question.

Those who scored within a range of 20 to 36 points on the index were identified as sympathetic respondents, and those scoring between 0 and 14 points were judged unsympathetic; respondents scoring in the narrow spread between 15 and 19 points were identified as uncommitted. The size of this group seems all the more significant because its members were drawn from a much smaller point segment of the index than were the sympathetic and unsympathetic sample groups. That this uncommitted or ambivalent group of Americans is so large is not surprising. Previous U.S. and European surveys on development-related issues[1] have also

---

[1] Alfred O. Hero, Jr., "American Public Reactions to Development Assistance" (Study prepared for the Brookings Institution Steering Committee on a possible new organization to develop U.S. public support for aid, Washington, D.C., 1968), p. 57; and Ruth Padrun, "Attitudes and Motivations of Manual Workers in Industry Concerning Development Issues," Report of an International Pilot Study prepared for Action for Development, of the U.N. Food and Agriculture Organization (Paris: International Institute of Research and Training in Education and Development, August 1972), p. 203.

shown a majority of public opinion (especially that of non-college, lower-income, uninformed respondents) to be marked by inconsistencies and internal contradictions.

In contrast to the significant number of Americans sympathetic to the concerns of the developing world, only 16 per cent of the U.S. national sample could be considered well informed. Thirty-six per cent of the respondents clearly were uninformed. The balance, 48 per cent, scoring in the intermediate range, were neither well informed nor grossly uninformed.

Figure VI-1. Development Sympathy of Respondents Related to Score on Information Index

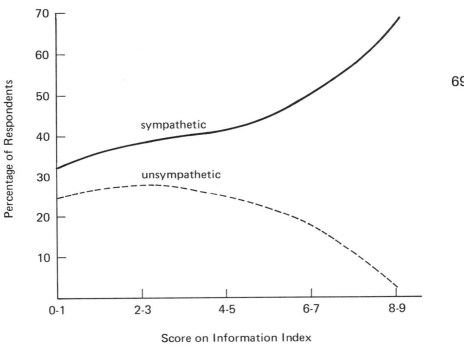

When sympathy is correlated with information, it becomes clear that those who are "informed" also exhibit a greater tendency to be "sympathetic." Figure VI-1 shows that 33 per cent of those respondents scoring zero or one on the information index also scored twenty points or more on the sympathy index. Thirty eight per cent of all respondents scoring two or three out of a possible nine points on the information index were sympathetic. Forty-one per cent of those respondents scoring four or five on the information index were sympathetic, while 50 per cent of the respondents scoring six and seven points on the information index were development sympathizers. Sixty-eight per cent of the best informed respondents (those scoring eight or nine on the information index) were sympathetic. When these values are plotted, it is obvious that a positive correlation exists between the degree to which a respondent is *informed* and the degree to which he is *sympathetic* on development issues. Figure VI-1 shows that there is a progressively greater percentage of sympathetic respondents among better informed groups; likewise there are fewer unsympathetic respondents among the better informed. Although the informed sample size is relatively small,[2] the cross-tabulation of sympathy and information scores indicates that sympathy is positively correlated with information (i.e., that it generally increases as information increases).[3]

This is not to say that a certain amount of information is the "cause" of an individual's sympathy on this set of issues, but rather that the relationship between information and sympathy is "non-random," or one that is more frequent than chance. It is clear from the data, however, that an American who is informed on development issues is more apt to be sympathetic on these same issues than is his uninformed peer. The question of how information on development affects development sympathy is of importance to the social scientist. But the matter of real relevance, especially for development educators, is that information and sympathy are closely related. To get a better reading on who the informed and sympathetic Americans are, these characteristics were cross-tabulated with a number of the standard demographic variables.

EDUCATION

The responses to this survey demonstrate that American attitudes on development issues are more directly a function of educational background than of any other single variable. This finding does not differ from those of earlier public opinion surveys. Alfred Hero's numerous studies of U.S. development assistance supporters led him to conclude that "level of education continues to be more closely associated with reactions to most types of nonmilitary aid than any other major demographic, social, or political variable."[4] The recent study, *State of the Nation*, conducted by Potomac Associates, points out that those Americans with "little education were among the least supportive of economic aid."[5]

European attitudes on these issues seem to be similarly influenced by formal educational training. Seventy-six per cent of all Swedes with university degrees support an increase in the Swedish aid budget, while only 23 per cent of elementary school graduates are so disposed.[6] The British Overseas Development Administra-

---

[2]See Annex C.

[3]This tendency has also been noted in a recent study of the development attitudes of European manual workers, which found that "the interviewees who are best informed are generally those who have a positive attitude toward underdeveloped countries . . . " The study cautioned, however, that information is not an independent variable; rather, it is often a function of education, age, political orientation, etc. See Ruth Padrun, "Attitudes and Motivations . . . ," p. 197.

[4]Alfred O. Hero, Jr., "American Public Reactions . . . ," p. 65.

[5]William Watts and Lloyd Free, *State of the Nation* (New York: Universe Books, 1973), p. 219.

[6]Stig Lindholm, *The Image of the Developing Countries: An Inquiry into Swedish Public Opinion* (Uppsala, Sweden: The Dag Hammarskjold Foundation, 1971), pp. 23 and 98.

tion's survey concludes that "attitudes towards Britain's giving help to the developing countries were very closely related to the informant's level of education," thus demonstrating "that the relationship between education and attitudes is a fundamental one."[7]

It is not surprising that those who are well informed on development issues are better educated than others. As Table VI-1

Table VI-1. Distribution of Informed Respondents According to Education

Education	Informed	All Others
Eighth Grade	10%	90%
Some High School	9	91
High School Graduates	12	88
Some College	15	85
Two Years College	19	81
College Graduates	27	73
Postgraduates	30	70

shows, the information level increases gradually as the degree to which a respondent is educated increases. What is quite striking is that those who have completed four years or more of university education are considerably better informed on development issues than all those with less than four years of college.

Table VI-2. Distribution of Sympathetic Respondents
According to Education

Education	Sympathetic	All Others
Eighth Grade	34%	66%
Some High School	34	66
High School Graduates	34	66
Some College	34	66
Two Years College	37	63
College Graduates	46	54
Postgraduates	56	44

A similar but stronger trend becomes apparent when sympathy is cross-tabulated with the level of education. All respondents with two years of college or less were sympathetic to virtually the same degree. However, four-year college graduates and respondents with postgraduate training exhibited a significantly higher degree of sympathy than did any other segment of the national sample. Thus education is a very significant, if not the most significant, correlate of development sympathy—as well as of development information. There appears to be an educational "threshold" at the four-year college graduate level, beyond which respondents exhibit a great deal more sympathy on development issues. As Table VI-2 shows, 37 per cent of all those with two years of

---

[7] I. Rauta, *Aid and Overseas Development: A Survey of Public Attitudes, Opinions and Knowledge* (London: Her Majesty's Stationery Office, 1971), pp. 7 and 64.

college were sympathetic on development issues, compared to 46 per cent of four-year graduates and 56 per cent of postgraduates. When age, party affiliation, and religion are held constant, the correlation between sympathy and education (especially for those with four years or more college education) is strongest. This correlation seems to be somewhat related to other demographic factors, particularly income and occupation.

Since higher education is an important distinguishing characteristic of development sympathy, one would expect sympathy to increase as the level of education in this country increases. In 1940, only 4.5 per cent of all Americans had completed college; in 1950, 6.0 per cent had done so; in 1960, 7.7 per cent; and in 1970, 11.0 per cent.[8]

INCOME

When all other factors are held the same, an individual's income is not as important a determinant of development sympathy as are his education or age. The income groups most sympathetic on global development issues are in the middle- to upper-middle-income sector, but there is no "constant" progression of sympathy

Table VI-3. Distribution of Sympathetic Respondents According to Income Level

Income	Sympathetic	All Others
Under $3,000	30%	70%
$3,000–$4,999	38	62
$5,000–$6,999	39	61
$7,000–$9,999	34	66
$10,000–$14,999	37	63
$15,000–$19,999	49	51
$20,000–$24,999	43	57
$25,000 and over	36	64

moving up the income ladder. Americans earning between $15,000 and $25,000 are the income groups most sympathetic to development problems and issues. Between these two, the $15,000–$19,999 sector exhibits the greatest degree of sympathy: 49 per cent of all respondents at this income level are sympathetic to international development. It should be noted that a disproportionately high percentage of this category is made up of university students who—according to standard survey practice—gave their parents' income level in response to the income query, as well as of young, highly educated professionals. It seems it is the high educational level of these groups, rather than their income, that determines their sympathetic development orientation. There is,

---

[8]U.S. Bureau of the Census, *Statistical Abstract of the United States: 1972*, 93rd ed. (Washington, D.C.: 1972).

however, some drop in the degree of sympathy in the $25,000 and over group, compared to the preceding two sectors; 36 per cent of respondents earning $25,000 and over are sympathetic, making this income group sixth in sympathy among the eight groups categorized. Similarly, the $25,000 and over category is second only to the $7,000-$9,999 group in having the greatest percentage (26 per cent) of unsympathetic respondents. As one might expect, the information index scores are higher in upper-income groups and lower at the other end of the income scale. The close relationship between income and formal education obviously accounts for much of this correlation.

From the income data obtained on those respondents who were unsympathetic, there is little evidence to suggest that lower-income Americans are more hostile to development concerns than higher-income Americans. It is clear, however, that there is a smaller percentage of "uncommitted" respondents in the upper-middle- and upper-income categories than in lower earning brackets. Such a tendency for better-educated (and therefore usually upper-income) groups to cluster or polarize at both extremes of an issue is a phenomenon familiar to social scientists.[9]

OCCUPATION AND UNION MEMBERSHIP

Throughout the survey data, students expectedly emerged as the group best informed and most sympathetic (54 per cent) on international development problems. Professionals (46 per cent), sales people (40 per cent), and civil servants (39 per cent) also exhibited high sympathy. Blue-collar workers were marginally less sympathetic, and farmers had the lowest percentage of development sympathizers among their ranks (28 per cent). While the group of respondents who characterized themselves as executives ranked fifth in sympathy (38 per cent) among the eight occupational

Table VI-4. Distribution of Informed Respondents
According to Occupation

Occupation	Informed	All Others
Student	37%	63%
Professional	25	75
Sales	24	76
Advertising/ Communications	20	80
Civil Service	16	84
Executive	14	86
Skilled Labor	14	86
Semi-Skilled	11	89
Farm	10	90
Other	10	90

[9]According to the cognitive consistency model, "increasing knowledge will change people in *different* directions leading to a greater polarization of opinion among the more knowledgable." See Andre Modigliani and William A. Gamson, "Knowledge and Foreign Policy Opinions," *Public Opinion Quarterly* 30 (Summer 1966), pp. 191-7.

**Table VI-5. Distribution of Sympathetic Respondents
According to Occupation**

Occupation	Sympathetic	All Others
Student	54%	46%
Professional	46	54
Sales	40	60
Civil Service	39	61
Executive	38	62
Skilled	35	65
Semi-Skilled	34	66
Advertising/ Communications	32	68
Farm	28	72
Other	34	66

groups, this group also scored first in the percentage of unsympathetic (31 per cent); thus there was again a notable polarization of highly educated groups at both extremes of the opinion spectrum. No occupational group could be characterized as particularly unsympathetic. American farmers, however, were notably uncommitted—perhaps because they tend to be less educated, less affluent, and older than other occupational groups.[10]

In general, white-collar workers demonstrated stronger sympathy than did blue-collar workers. In contrast to the differences in sympathy between white- and blue-collar workers, the comparative data this survey turned up on union and non-union household attitudes may be somewhat surprising to any readers expecting to find the "hard hat" syndrome operative on international development issues. As we saw in the case of trade issues and as Table VI-6 indicates, there is no significant difference in the level of information or degree of sympathy of these two groups.

**Table VI-6. Distribution of Sympathetic and Informed Respondents
by Union Membership**

	Sympathy		Information	
	Sympathetic	All Others	Informed	All Others
Union Households	40%	60%	17%	83%
Non-Union Households	37	63	15	85

AGE

The lines of division are somewhat clearer between different age groups. Young people (eighteen to twenty-five years of age) unquestionably comprise the group of Americans best informed about development (22 per cent, or 6 percentage points above the national average) and most sympathetic to development (47 per cent, or 9 percentage points over the national average). Those

---

[10] Farmers have the lowest average weekly earnings of any American occupational group except for household workers, and 69 per cent are over 44 years of age compared to only 30 per cent of the nation's total population. See *Statistical Abstract: 1972*, p. 231-3.

forty-six to fifty-five years of age have fewer development sympathizers within their ranks (31 per cent, or 7 percentage points below the national average) and more individuals who are not sympathetic (34 per cent, or 9 percentage points above the national average) than any other group of Americans. Conversely, the group of eighteen to twenty-five year olds is 7 percentage points below the national average in the number of individuals within its fold who are not sympathetic.

While young people are the most sympathetic segment of the American public, this predisposition is not simply a function of youth but also of education. The disparities between youth and adult attitudes narrow somewhat when adult positions are compared only to non-college youth. Nevertheless, those who are eighteen to twenty-five years old are still more sympathetic than any other population grouping regardless of educational background. However, the degree to which any group of Americans over twenty-five years of age is more sympathetic is a function of education more than it is of age.

Young Americans historically have been more supportive of nonmilitary aid than their elders—with people over fifty years of age being least supportive. This is no doubt partly a function of the negative relationship of education with age; older Americans are less educated than younger Americans. Although past surveys showed this correlation of age and aid support to be much weaker when education was held constant, they nevertheless showed support to be stronger among young people than among adults.[11] In this survey, the development sympathy shown by young Americans is partly due to the prevalence of university background within this group. With education held constant, some of the differences between youth and adult attitudes blur.

75

POLITICAL PARTY

Americans who regard themselves as political "Independents" are more likely to be advocates of U.S. development support than members of any other political group. In development sympathy, the two major political parties follow a good distance behind the Independents (48 per cent), with Democrats second (40 per cent), and Republicans last (33 per cent, or five percentage points below the national average).

When party membership is cross-tabulated with age, it becomes clear that young party members generally are most favorably disposed toward development issues, while older members are least so. Older Republicans (56 years of age or older) are least oriented toward helping poor countries, while young Independents are most supportive of such assistance. Similarly, the attitudinal differences between parties within the group eighteen to twenty-five years old are rather small, whereas among older groups these variations are considerably greater.

Cross-tabulations of sympathy and party, with education held constant, once again reveal that, while some attitudinal differences do exist between members of different parties irrespective of educational background, education is clearly the most important

---

[11] Alfred O. Hero, Jr., "American Public Reactions . . . ," p. 72.

Table VI-7. Distribution of Sympathetic Respondents According to Political Party Affiliation[a]

Party	Sympathetic	All Others
Democrat	40%	60%
Republican	33	67
Independent	48	52
Other	47	53

[a]Actual U.S. political party membership in 1968: Democrat, 45 per cent; Republican, 24 per cent; Independent, 30 per cent. Source: Survey Research Center, University of Michigan, Ann Arbor, Michigan.

determinant. On the information index, both Independents and Republicans scored higher than Democratic party members; this is probably a function of the very different demographic profiles of the two major U.S. political parties, especially with regard to education.

POLITICAL ORIENTATION

Over three quarters of all Americans who are development sympathizers consider themselves politically moderate or left of moderate. Conservatives are much more negatively disposed toward increasing U.S. support for international development efforts.

Those interviewed were presented with a card showing a scale of political views ranging from "radical left" to "ultra-conservative." Each respondent then was asked to place himself somewhere on the nine-point scale. While most Americans consider themselves politically "moderate" (41 per cent), more respondents see themselves as "conservative" (15 per cent) than "liberal" (11 per cent). All respondents who ranked themselves left of "moderate" comprise 24 per cent of the national sample, and those who ranked themselves to the right of "moderate," 27 per cent.

Table VI-8. Self-Ranking of Respondents on Political Orientation Scale[a]

Radical Left		Liberal		Moderate		Conservative		Ultra-Conservative
1	2	3	4	5	6	7	8	9
2%	3%	11%	8%	41%	9%	15%	2%	1%
24%				27%				

[a]Eight per cent of respondents were unsure of their political leaning.

It is interesting that on the information index, there was no difference between the average scores of all those to the left of moderate and all those to the right of moderate. The "ultra-conservative" group scored highest on development information, with the group just to the right of radical left scoring second best informed. Of course, this does not necessarily mean that information breeds politicization; it is just as plausible that politicization

Table VI-9. Distribution of Sympathetic Respondents According to Political Orientation

Political Orientation (scale from 1 to 9)	Sympathetic	All Others
1. Radical Left	46%	54%
2. Left of Liberal	72	28
3. Liberal	49	51
4. Moderate-Liberal	44	56
5. Moderate	39	61
6. Moderate-Conservative	31	69
7. Conservative	32	68
8. Right of Conservative	8	92
9. Ultra-Conservative	5	95

feeds the desire for information. Those respondents who characterized themselves as "moderate" (41 per cent) placed next to last on the information index, while the radical group scored lowest.

The results were markedly different in the case of the sympathy index. The 24 per cent of the American public that considers itself to the left of moderate is very significantly more sympathetic on development issues than the 27 per cent of the nation ranked to the right of moderate. As Table VI-9 shows, the group with the highest percentage of development sympathizers (72 per cent) is just to the left of "liberal." Only 5 per cent of those Americans who consider themselves "ultra-conservative" are sympathetic. These same two groups also have, respectively, the lowest and highest percentages of unsympathetic respondents.

RELIGION

Since religious groups traditionally have been considered a very important component of any U.S. development constituency, we examined the relationship of religion to sympathy and information in relatively greater detail. A good deal of traditional support for development has been generated through "moral" appeals. Indeed, the results of this survey, too, show that for most Americans, the basic rationale for development support is still moral and humanitarian concern. Some U.S. churches have devoted resources to informing their members on global poverty issues. Furthermore, European surveys suggest positive correlations between religious commitment and development support.[12] We therefore pursued this question with great interest.

The composition of the American public by religion is as follows: Protestant, 35 per cent; Catholic, 24 per cent; Jewish, 3 per cent; and other affiliations, 38 per cent. Of the three major U.S. religious groups, Jewish Americans are best informed, fol-

---

[12]See "Memorandum on a Community Policy on Development Cooperation" (Brussels: Commission of the European Communities, 1972), pp. 107-8.

lowed by Protestants and Catholics—a ranking that once again is probably attributable to social and economic factors rather than to religious training.[13] According to the sympathy index, 54 per cent of all Jewish Americans, 49 per cent of those not falling within any of the three major religious groups, 39 per cent of Catholics, and 35 per cent of Protestants are development sympathizers.

The survey data reveal that religious influence is in fact an insignificant factor in explaining an individual's level of information or disposition toward development issues. Table VI-10 shows that the degree to which a respondent claimed religion had influenced his life made little difference in the way he viewed development issues. Forty-one per cent of all respondents who indicated that religion exerted a "strong" influence on their lives were sympathetic, while 39 per cent of those for whom religion represented "hardly any" influence were sympathetic—an insignificant difference. The percentages of development sympathizers among those who said religion influenced them "a great deal" and those who said it influenced them "somewhat" were similarly indistinguishable—36 per cent and 35 per cent, respectively. This finding contrasts sharply with data on European attitudes, which do suggest a positive correlation between religious commitment and support for development assistance.[14]

Table VI-10. Distribution of Sympathetic Respondents According to Degree of Religious Influence

Influenced by Religion	Sympathetic	All Others
Strongly	41%	59%
Great deal	36	64
Somewhat	35	65
Hardly any	39	61
Unsure	34	66

RACE

Although white respondents were somewhat more informed on development issues (17 per cent) than black respondents (10 per cent), the latter were more sympathetic (44 per cent compared to 37 per cent). This may seem surprising, since domestic poverty and urban issues are assumed by many to be the only concerns of blacks. Although the relatively higher development sympathy score of blacks is due to their response to the first question on the sympathy index—their strong feeling that government should

---

[13]Though the actual size of the Jewish sample was quite small and somewhat homogenous, the trends discussed above are, nevertheless, still consistent with previous survey data. See Alfred O. Hero, Jr., *American Religious Groups View Foreign Policy* (Durham, N.C.: Duke University Press, 1973), p. 62.

[14]Commission of the European Communities, "Memorandum . . . ," p. 107-8.

spend more to fight poverty at home—blacks are also more sympathetic than average on international poverty issues. A more significant difference is evident concerning unsympathetic sentiment. Only 12 per cent of blacks are negatively disposed toward development issues, whereas 27 per cent of whites are unsympathetic. The survey data indicate, then, that the black population is relatively more sympathetic on development issues, and definitely less negative or unsympathetic (14 per cent less) than the white population.

SEX

Although American men (18 per cent) are somewhat more informed on development issues than women (13 per cent)—a function, no doubt, of their different levels of formal educational training—there is virtually no difference between the two groups in development sympathy: 37 per cent of the male respondents and 38 per cent of the female respondents are development sympathizers. Sex is clearly not an important determinant in support of or opposition to development concerns.

79

TRAVEL

Finally, each respondent was asked a series of questions regarding overseas travel—how much time was spent traveling outside the United States, where, and for what purpose—in the expectation that some correlation would be found between travel to the developing world and development sympathy. Surprisingly, no such correlation was evident. The reasons are not altogether clear, but perhaps the travel habits of most Americans are so insular that no real change in consciousness is effected by visits to the developing world.

CONCLUSION

The analysis of the sympathy and information indices provides some indication of how knowledgeable and committed Americans are on poverty and development issues. Almost two of every five Americans (38 per cent) can be considered strong development sympathizers, while 25 per cent are firm opponents. Perhaps more important, an additional 37 per cent are uncommitted but not negatively disposed; this relatively large group clearly includes potential supporters of international development.

Those Americans who are young, college-educated, middle- to upper-middle–income bracket, white-collar, and politically either Independents or Democrats judging themselves to be to the left of moderate are most likely to be development supporters. Older, less-educated, lower-income, blue-collar, and politically conservative Americans are generally among those who oppose U.S. development support. The 37 per cent of the public identified as uncommitted an global development issues combines some of the characteristics of both groups. Sex, union membership, and religious affiliation are factors which largely do not determine an American's predisposition on global development issues.

In general, Americans are not well informed on global poverty problems, the people and nations of the developing world, or the meager U.S. response to the latter's problems. According to the results of this survey, only 16 per cent of the people of this country can be considered well informed on these issues, while 36 per cent are quite poorly informed. However, some 48 per cent of the American populace—almost one out of every two people—falls somewhere between the two extremes. Taken together, the demonstrated correlation between information and sympathy and the fact that 37 per cent of the public remains uncommitted make it quite clear that effective development education programs would increase U.S. understanding of development issues, and therefore probably increase the degree of development support.

toward greater support for development

The study so far has identified two key groups of Americans that are of importance to all those concerned with U.S. foreign policy and American relations with the developing countries: the 38 per cent of the American public that is sympathetic with the concerns and needs of the poor countries and the 37 per cent that is ambivalent and uncommitted on these issues. As shown in Chapter VI, the two groups have rather different characteristics. The "sympathetic" American tends to be a better-educated, more prosperous white-collar worker, while his "ambivalent" counterpart is likely to have only a high school education and a lower income.

81

Which is the key group to reach if one is interested in eliciting a more generous American response to the needs of the poor countries? There is no simple answer. It can be argued that development education programs aimed at the development "sympathizers" are a far more valid and politically effective use of scarce resources to intensify and marshall the existing support for development programs. It certainly is true that, in the short run, political support for more liberal development policies will have to come from the politically active and articulate minority among the sympathizers.

Yet over the longer period, the broader support that will be necessary to redirect national and international priorities must come as well from that group which this survey has identified as "ambivalent." It is this group, added to those who are already sympathetic to development problems, that can provide the potential support for the types of policies that must be created if the United States is to be genuinely responsive to the problems of the poor countries.

The choice of working with the sympathetic or with the ambivalent audience is up to the organizations concerned. However, the results of the survey show that education strategies will differ according to that choice. Therefore, this chapter will discuss the role of education and information in generating development support, as well as what channels of communication can be utilized to best advantage in various development education programs. It will also examine current and proposed U.S. policies in light of what the survey shows about the likelihood of their support by the public.

THE ROLE OF DEVELOPMENT INFORMATION

The survey findings analyzed in previous chapters show that Americans who are informed about development and poverty are more apt to be sympathetic on development issues than those who are uninformed. Conversely, greater percentages of the uninformed public than of the informed public are unsympathetic on development issues. What is significant for the development educator is that increased public knowledge about poverty and development issues is a key aspect of development support. The logical conclusion, therefore, is that programs which raise the knowledge level of Americans on poverty and development issues will have the effect of increasing development support.

Responses to two conditional survey questions further underscore the importance of information to development support. These questions sought to determine, among other things, whether or not providing additional information on specific development issues would change public opinion on those issues; and if so, which segments of the American public would be most likely to change their views. After answering how they would allocate the U.S. budget for domestic and international poverty programs, respondents were asked to reconsider their answers on the basis of the following statement: "If you were told that 95 per cent of the poor people in the world lived in other countries, and the United States had only 5 per cent of the world's poor, would you reconsider your distribution of money (to domestic and international poverty programs)?" Twenty-six per cent of the respondents said they would reconsider allocating the budget (as Table II-11, p. 18 indicates). Only 19 per cent of the college-graduate respondents said they would reconsider compared to 29 per cent of all high school graduates. More than half of those who reconsidered (53 per cent) said they would divide the poverty budget "proportionately so that most of it would go to help the poor in other parts of the world," and another 34 per cent said they would choose to divide the budget "about fifty-fifty between the poor of the United States and the poor in other parts of the world." These results demonstrate that a significantly large group of Americans—especially those without college education—are willing to change and even reverse their opinion on a development issue when provided with factual information relevant to forming an opinion on that issue.

A similar shift of opinion also was evident in another series of questions. After expressing his position on import restrictions, each individual was asked to consider a list of basic arguments in support of and in opposition to freer trade with the poor countries. The respondent was then asked: "Now that you have read some of the arguments about free trade with underdeveloped countries, would you say you basically favor or oppose it?" Although only 2 per cent of the respondents subsequently shifted their position to favor free trade, 10 per cent fewer were now opposed to such a policy, and an additional 9 per cent became unsure of their original position. The shift in response among those who were high school graduates was even more conspicuous. Fifty-four per cent of this group initially opposed freer trade with the poor countries, but only 38 per cent maintained this position after reading the arguments, and 26 per cent (compared to 13 per cent initially) stated they were unsure of their position after reconsidering (see Table IV-4, p. 56).

Those Americans who changed their opinions on these conditional questions were by and large part of the 37 per cent of the public which this survey has identified as having unformed, ambivalent opinions on development. Clearly this large, uncommitted group of Americans has given little thought to global poverty questions. We also know that most of this ambivalent group is not predisposed *against* assisting underdeveloped countries, but is uninformed about global poverty and development issues. We can therefore assume that vigorous education campaigns targeted at this audience could significantly increase public support for more positive U.S. policies aimed at assisting the poor countries.

CHANNELS OF COMMUNICATION

What are the best channels of communication for reaching large groups of Americans with a message about international development issues? Where does the public get its information on world problems? To whom or to what sources do Americans turn for objective facts and fair analyses? How do the people of this country form their judgments on matters of foreign affairs?

As we have seen, the survey results show that Americans are short on the "facts" of foreign policy—or at least of international development. Only 16 per cent of the public scored high enough on the information index to be judged "informed." More than one out of every three (36 per cent) Americans scored zero on the information index. Another 48 per cent of the public ranked somewhere between these two extremes. Only 22 per cent of the American public was able to select from five widely differing multiple choices the approximate percentage of the world's population living in underdeveloped countries! Thus, whatever the sources to which it presently turns for information, the American public is either getting a lean diet of development information or not digesting what it does receive.

The survey respondents were provided with a list of thirteen sources of information for "learning about the various problems in the world." They were asked if these sources are "very important," "somewhat important," or "not important." The responses show that Americans unquestionably consider television to be a very important source of information on world problems. There are some significant differences, however, in the relative importance assigned to television by various groups of the public. For example, 68 per cent of high school graduates, compared to 54 per cent of college graduates, regard it a "very important" source of information. Significant disparities are also evident in a comparison of sources identified as important by informed and uninformed Americans. Almost two thirds (65 per cent) of uninformed Americans, compared to 59 per cent of the informed group, con-

Table VII-1. Relative Importance Attributed to Various Information Sources

	Very Important	Somewhat Important	Not Important	Not Sure
Television	64%	29%	6%	1%
Newspapers	62	31	7	—
Radio	42	41	16	1
School	40	34	22	4
Personal Experience	33	36	26	5
Books	30	40	27	3
Family	28	38	31	3
Magazines	25	43	28	4
Friends	21	45	33	2
Work Experience	25	32	38	5
Church	23	36	38	3
Pamphlets & Newsletters	16	40	39	5
Special Meetings	12	29	53	6

sider television a "very important" source of information. A considerably greater percentage of informed (68 per cent) than of uninformed (57 per cent) Americans regards newspapers as "very important." Similarly, more college graduates rank newspapers (65 per cent) rather than television (54 per cent) as a "very important" source.

Respondents were also asked to indicate which sources of information they judged to be among the "most reliable" and which among the "least reliable." Again, informed and college-graduate Americans were much less trusting of television information than were the uninformed and high school graduates. While more than half of all informed (54 per cent) and college-graduate

Table VII-2. Information Sources Considered "Most Reliable"[a]

	Television	Newspapers	Radio	School	Personal Experience
Total	**64%**	**52%**	**27%**	**13%**	**17%**
Education					
College Graduates	51	50	16	19	17
Some College	56	52	24	17	25
High School Graduates	68	53	27	12	17
Non-High School Graduates	72	53	33	9	11
Age					
18-25	61	49	23	20	23
26-35	65	55	28	15	18
36-50	61	49	27	10	17
Over 50	65	54	29	9	10
Income					
Upper	56	51	24	17	19
Middle	65	53	25	14	19
Lower	69	51	32	8	13
Blacks	77	45	35	13	14

[a]Totals add up to more than 100 per cent because respondents could give several answers.

(51 per cent) Americans consider television a "most reliable" source of information, two thirds of the uninformed (66 per cent) and high school graduates (68 per cent) give it this ranking. Almost the same percentages of informed respondents place newspapers and television among the "most reliable" sources of information (52 per cent and 54 per cent, respectively). Uninformed individuals, however, have a sharply different view—with 66 per cent ranking television and only 46 per cent ranking newspapers as "most reliable." Similarly large disparities exist between the responses of high school (68 per cent television, 53 per cent newspapers) and college graduates (51 per cent television, 50 per cent newspapers).

Table VII-3. Relative Importance and Reliability Attributed to Information Sources by Informed and Uninformed Respondents[a]

	Informed			Uninformed		
	Very Important	Most Reliable	Least Reliable	Very Important	Most Reliable	Least Reliable
Television	59%	54%	0%	65%	66%	0%
Newspapers	68	52	0	57	46	0
Radio	40	22	0	43	28	0
School	43	15	0	35	10	0
Books	38	16	0	22	6	0
Magazines	35	19	0	18	7	5
Personal Experience	33	26	11	29	11	17
Work Experience	28	11	23	23	5	17
Family	25	7	0	31	9	0
Friends	21	5	6	22	3	10
Pamphlets & Newsletters	18	3	22	11	3	10
Church	15	12	16	27	11	7
Meetings	11	4	15	10	3	14

[a]Note that the answers of 48 per cent of respondents falling between the "informed" and "uninformed" are not shown in this table.

The "school" and "radio" rank next as important and reliable sources of information, with radio considered among the "most reliable" by more people (27 per cent) than school (13 per cent). High school graduates (27 per cent) and uninformed individuals (28 per cent) attribute more reliability to radio than do college graduates (16 per cent) or the informed (22 per cent). Moreover, school was listed as a "very important" source more frequently by informed individuals (43 per cent) than by the uninformed (35 per cent). It should be noted, nevertheless, that *all* groups consider television and newspapers to be by far the most important and reliable sources of information. All other source rankings and evaluations should be understood in that context.

A number of other differences in the importance and reliability of sources of information are evident between the informed and college educated on the one hand, and the uninformed and high school educated on the other. Most notably, books and magazines are considered "very important" sources of information by a little more than a third of the informed group but by less than a

Table VII-4. Information Sources Considered "Least Reliable"[a]

	Friends	Pamphlets & Newsletters	Special Meetings	Magazines	Church	Newspapers	Family	Work Experience
Total	**34%**	**30%**	**22%**	**17%**	**16%**	**16%**	**14%**	**14%**
Education								
College Graduates	36	31	27	8	22	13	18	8
Some College	38	28	24	12	21	19	15	13
High School Graduates	39	30	18	16	15	17	14	15
Non-High School Graduates	27	32	22	25	13	15	13	15
Age								
18-25	41	26	20	11	26	16	20	15
26-35	44	30	20	17	16	14	16	15
36-50	28	31	25	18	14	19	13	13
Over 50	28	33	22	20	11	16	10	12

[a]Totals add up to more than 100 per cent because respondents could give several answers.

fourth of the uninformed group. Similarly, books and magazines are considered "very important" by more than a third of college graduates, but by considerably less than a third of high school graduates. Whereas informed Americans rank books and magazines fifth and sixth in both importance and reliability, the uninformed list these information sources tenth and eleventh in importance. Similarly, 21 per cent of all college graduates, but only 8 per cent of high school graduates, regard books as a reliable source.

The public does not consider the churches an important or reliable source of information on world problems, although here, too, there are differences between the responses of various segments of the public. Thus while the uninformed group ranks the churches seventh in importance among thirteen sources, informed Americans rank churches next to last. Similarly, while 15 per cent of high school graduates consider the churches among the "least reliable" sources, 22 per cent of the college-educated public places churches in this category. While 7 per cent of the responses of the uninformed consider the churches to be a "least reliable" source of information, 16 per cent of informed Americans give them this ranking.

HOW TO INCREASE PUBLIC SUPPORT

While some world affairs education programs have continued to rely upon traditional communication techniques (such as meetings and pamphlets), others have searched without success for the "perfect" medium. There is no set of education media that is especially effective for communicating on *development* issues, as distinct from other issues. Those channels that most effectively reach large audiences with a message on urban problems, for example, will also be most effective in communicating on development.

The essence of any message likely to interest the American public in world poverty and development issues would have to communicate the seriousness of global poverty problems, the prospects for their solution, as well as the present and potential U.S. role in alleviating them. The survey shows that development information programs will more easily engage the public's interest by examining the relationship between domestic and international concerns. Similarly, information showing the interdependence of the United States and the poor countries would increase understanding of how U.S. assistance for underdeveloped countries is in our interest and could contribute to greater development support.

The Media

Because more Americans consider television and newspapers to be the most important and reliable sources of information, the use of these media will do most to build broad public understanding and support on development issues. At the very least, such means will be more effective in reaching more people than will special meetings, pamphlets, newsletters, and the churches.

Americans give television, newspapers, and radio high marks on importance and reliability because these sources provide "on the scene, quick, up-to-date, consistent, and complete" reporting of the facts. In short, Americans like to be presented with what they believe are "objective" facts so that they can form their own opinions. Attempts to "package" and "bias" the facts are not appreciated—if they are recognized. The obvious power of the media—and television specifically—is also evident in survey responses to questions relating to country recognition. China emerged in the survey as the second best known country on a list of seventeen—after a period of over twenty years during which exposure to China, as well as public discussion about that country, had been minimal. The President's trip (taken some eight months before the survey field work) and the media coverage it generated obviously changed public awareness dramatically.

In contrast, a few of the less developed countries that have been in the news more than others have scored low on the recognition scale. Thus Bangladesh ranks second among nations most favored for assistance, but also second on the list of countries about which *least is known.* This suggests that Americans have a general perception, probably from television, of the magnitude of the problems in Bangladesh but know little more about it. Media coverage, then, has played an effective role in identifying "dramatic" problems or events, but not in providing the public with much background information regarding development and poverty issues. One can speculate that different countries will be more visible to the public at different times, depending on world events. Had this survey, for example, been conducted shortly after the widespread news coverage of the *coup d'etat* in Chile, one would expect that Americans would have been more familiar with that country than they were at the time of our field work.

Communication with college-educated Americans, who are more apt than others to be informed and sympathetic on development issues, can also be achieved through newspapers, magazines, and books. As has been noted in recent analyses of American information sources, "radio and television seem to serve a key role in signalizing events, in which they announce the immediate—and usually sketchy—reports of a happening. But much news is left out by the broadcast media, leaving to the newspapers the important task of supplying the details."[1] Books and magazines also perform a similar role of supplying background and detailed information on an issue—particularly for informed and well-educated Americans. While 38 per cent and 35 per cent of the group identified by the survey as "informed" regarded books and magazines, respectively, as "very important" information sources, only 22 per cent and 18 per cent, respectively, of the uninformed sample agreed (see Table VII-3). Thus the printed media are relatively far less important than television in drawing nationwide attention to a problem, but seem to have an important role in helping the educated public better understand and evaluate news items.

Youth and the Schools

No educational program seeking to inform Americans and shape their attitudes can ignore society's main socializing institution—the school. This is especially true with regard to development issues,

---

[1] "Best Informed Voters Prefer Print Media," *Editor and Publisher* (April 7, 1973), p. 7.

since this study has identified youth as the segment of the American public that is most sympathetic to development concerns. Young Americans—those eighteen to twenty-five years old—regard school as their most important source of information on world problems after television and newspapers. Fifty-two per cent of American youth regards school as a "very important" information source. It follows, then, that were development to become a more central focus of curricular and extra-curricular activities, youth's strong development support would increase. Such a prospect would argue well for the introduction of information on global poverty and development issues into school curricula. Similarly, the secondary school and university community environments should offer an ideal setting for informal development education programs—given the availability of educational resources, a sympathetic adult audience, and leisure time available to young people for such programs.

Citizen Groups

While the traditional world affairs communication channels—special meetings, pamphlets, and newsletters—may be effective in reaching those Americans who already are concerned with foreign policy issues, they will not reach the uninvolved public. If the aim is to expand the development constituency, use of such methods will not succeed. All groups—informed or not, well-educated or not, sympathetic or unsympathetic—considered special meetings, pamphlets, and newsletters to be "not important" and "least reliable" sources of information. In reply to the open-ended question about why respondents regarded these sources to be among the "least reliable," most stated that special meetings and pamphlets are "biased and prejudiced" sources providing one with "opinionated" and "exaggerated" views of the truth. Despite these findings, citizen groups whose resources and program opportunities limit them to use of special meetings, pamphlets, and newsletters could more effectively reach their constituencies by improving these channels of communication. Programs and publications that the public judges more objective and open to opposing points of view, and less peremptory and slanted, will have greater prospects for affecting public attitudes. For instance, use of the local media by these organizations provides an excellent opportunity for reaching a broader public with information and education on poverty and development issues. In addition, adding a broader development focus to their existing work with the local schools could improve community awareness on international issues.

Citizen groups are obviously important to any program aimed at generating short-term support for development policies, since the constituencies of these groups tend to be comprised of well-educated and politically active Americans. These community education organizations can also play a vital long-term role in generating increased development support by providing the intellectual depth and leadership on development issues that are necessary for better public understanding and support.

The Churches

The 16 per cent of all Americans who regard the churches to be among the "least reliable" sources of information explained their position by their feeling that the churches provide biased and exaggerated views of world problems. Almost two of every five (38 per cent) Americans consider the churches a "not important" information source, placing them tenth in importance among the thirteen sources considered by respondents. It should be noted, however, that this low ranking is not assigned the churches by black Americans.

It seems ironic, indeed, that Americans perceive the churches to be playing a very insignificant leadership role in helping to form and direct national consciousness on what are ultimately major issues of global ethics. Few leadership groups have as many opportunities for communicating with large segments of the public as do clergymen. It would seem most appropriate for churchmen to assume a central leadership role in developing the global consciousness necessary to build policies of development support. Since Americans respond to development concerns largely out of moral and humanitarian instincts—the direct province of organized religion—it seems logical for the churches to assert greater national leadership on issues of global development.

Black Americans

This survey has found that the black population is somewhat more sympathetic and considerably less negative toward development issues than the white population of similar economic standing. The black population should therefore be seen as a potential source of development support. The survey results show that while only 23 per cent of the total U.S. population regards the churches as "very important" information sources on world problems, 43 per cent of all blacks give them this ranking. Blacks also see the churches as a more reliable source of information than do other Americans. Another dramatic difference is evident with regard to "the family" as a source of information on world problems. Forty-three per cent of all blacks, compared to 28 per cent of the population as a whole, consider the family a "very important" information source. Television and radio, too, are more important sources of information on world problems to blacks than they are to the general public. Over three out of four blacks (77 per cent) consider television a "very important" source of information compared to 64 per cent of the total national sample. Half of all blacks regard radio as a "very important" information source (compared to 42 per cent of the general public). To strengthen the already favorable orientation of blacks to development, educators could best reach this audience through the churches, as well as through those electronic media outlets which have a wide audience among blacks.

Personal and Work Experience

Since personal experience and (to a lesser extent) work experience are considered to be relatively important and reliable sources of information, they provide substantial room for creative development education programming. This survey suggests that the involvement of Americans in leisure or work-related activities with a development orientation bears real prospects for increasing public interest in development. Such activities might include international entertainment for workers at lunch-time, simulation games related to employment or consumer experience, articles targeted for specific professional groups relating development to medicine or law, advertising, or agriculture. The success of such educational activities might profitably be monitored by taking short community surveys before and after the activities.

It is clear, then, that there is a multiplicity of ways to better educate Americans about poverty and development issues. The methods that are effective with some groups are ill-suited for communicating with others. Yet, however development educators choose to reach the public with information about development, according to the survey, certain U.S. policy changes are necessary for expanding development support among the American people.

WHAT POLICIES WILL AMERICANS SUPPORT?

The great temptation for U.S. foreign policy makers is to rationalize that current development policy is commensurate with what public opinion will sustain. Given the current low ebb in U.S. development support, one would expect Americans to be more opposed to international development efforts at present than ever before. Our survey results suggest that such a conclusion about the present situation is far off the mark.

There is little doubt, of course, that official U.S. support for development has plummeted in the last decade. A recent United Nations report on the implementation of the General Assembly—approved International Development Strategy chides the developed countries for their failure to help create policies conducive to accelerating development in the poor countries. The report states that the most conspicuous cause of the sluggish response of industrialized nations' participation in the strategy has been the "diminishing effort by the United States."[2] Erosion of its share of financial aid has been "not more than offset" by the other advanced market economies. Similarly, the Development Assistance Committee (DAC) of the Organization for Economic Cooperation and Development now ranks the United States fourteenth among the sixteen industrialized nations in terms of share of GNP devoted to official development assistance; and the recent U.S. government's responses on commodity agreements, trade preferences, and support for multilateral lending institutions have been equally disappointing. At a time when other donor nations are significantly increasing their contributions to the international financial institutions, the United States—by promising, at best, to maintain previous levels of commitment—is dragging its feet on the implementation of the spirit and letter of the International Development Strategy.

Yet our survey data indicate that American public support for greater development cooperation is higher now, when we are

[2] United Nations, *Report of the Committee for Development Planning* (E/5293), May 1973.

actually doing less, than it was when we were doing much more in the decades of the 1950s and 1960s. Not only do more Americans than ever before support the proposition that the United States should be providing development assistance, but at the very time when official U.S. government assistance has been declining, voluntary development assistance from the American people has risen to an all-time high. In 1971, voluntary contributions from the American public amounted to $889.6 million, or 66 per cent of total international voluntary aid. U.S. voluntary contributions (.06 per cent of GNP) were second only to those of Sweden (.07 per cent) and significantly above the average of .04 per cent.[3]

How, then, do policy makers get their signals? Which publics are they listening to? A concise answer to the question of how public opinion affects policy is difficult to provide. On the one hand, it is obvious that public opinion has *some* impact, simply because policy makers state they consider it a matter of continuing concern. On the other hand, it is not at all clear what the precise effect may be in the case of any individual issue. Moreover, the impact of public opinion on *foreign* policy is different from the impact of opinion on issues which directly affect the local or state level. There is a lack of well-defined channels by which policy makers can find out what public opinion may be on foreign policy issues.

Past studies of opinion influence make it all too clear that policy makers rely on a varied set of imperfect mechanisms to find out what Americans are thinking. In many cases, the key factor may not be what American public opinion actually *is*, but what policy makers in the Executive and Legislative branches of the federal government *think it is.* James Rosenau in a 1963 study of American opinion makers and public foreign policy support states: "Whatever their generalized images of the public may be, apparently opinion makers do equate the direction and growth of their own attitudes with those of the public's insofar as specific issues are concerned."[4] Yet when current American policies are contrasted with the attitudes of the American public indicated in this survey, it becomes obvious that there are few other issues of public policy today on which the perceptions of the policy makers are so different from the actual sentiments of the American people.

From the results of the survey, it is clear that the American public has not become "isolationist," and Americans do not desire to withdraw from active participation in the outside world. Of course, Americans are interested in seeing domestic problems dealt with before turning to international problems, but this has always been true—although the feeling appears to be stronger at present

---

[3] While the OECD figures for voluntary assistance include foundation and corporate grants, U.S. Agency for International Development figures for voluntary assistance exclusive of such grants show more dramatic increases in voluntary aid. Overall U.S. voluntary aid shows a ten-year increase of 60 per cent even excluding aid to Israel. See Report by the Chairman of the Development Assistance Committee, *Development Co-operation, 1972 Review* (Paris: OECD, 1972), p. 66.

[4] James Rosenau, *Domestic Sources of Foreign Policy* (New York: Free Press, 1967), p. 237.

Figure VII-1. Ten Year Trend in U.S. Official and Voluntary Development Assistance

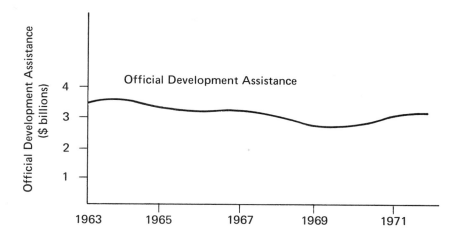

Official Development Assistance

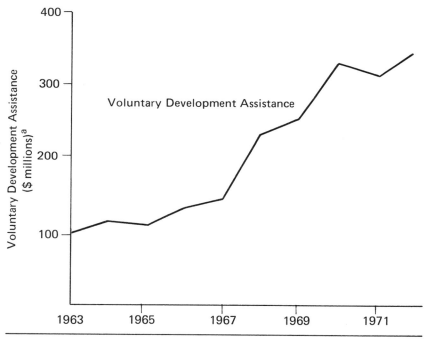

Voluntary Development Assistance

[a]Supplies and funds

than previously. This does not mean, however, that the public is unconcerned about the problems of development and the developing countries.

The survey results also show that Americans lack even a basic understanding of the absolute problem of poverty and misery that faces three quarters of the world's population on a daily basis. Yet despite this lack of concrete information, they express a strong degree of sympathy for the problems of the developing countries. Moreover, the survey shows that opinions can be changed when Americans are provided with relevant information.

This finding highlights the importance of national leadership on development issues. Whether in the Legislative or Executive branch, policy makers have a great deal of latitude to advocate and carry out policies that are genuinely responsive to the needs of the poor countries—without suffering any losses on election day. Such policies would engender no strong opposition and, with the proper leadership, could even gain a substantial degree of positive public support. However, it is also clear that this support will not come about unless positive steps are taken both inside and outside the government to mobilize public opinion.

There are caveats, however, to the above observations. The survey results indicate that in the public's view, domestic concerns will continue to take priority. Most congressmen thus will be hard put to support programs aimed at alleviating international poverty as long as there is a lag in the attack on serious domestic economic and social problems. Therefore those who favor more positive policies toward the developing countries must ensure that domestic social problems are dealt with at the same time. Furthermore, on certain issues, the views of small but articulate minorities will be important. Trade issues are one conspicuous example. More liberal trade policies toward poor countries currently are being opposed by a substantial segment of the American labor leadership. However, the survey indicates that the American people as a whole do not share this view.

The United States is now entering a period when it must make a number of new decisions which are likely to shape future cooperation between the developed and developing countries.[5] Prominent among these is the need to redesign U.S. aid programs—both bilateral and multilateral. Recent efforts to restructure a diminishing bilateral aid effort and to focus our assistance on the poorest majority in the developing countries are a welcome step. Policy makers should realize, if they have not already, that a rationale for aid grounded in military security is basically very weak. Americans no longer see the possibility of developing countries "going communist" as a threat to national security. Likewise, there is essentially no support for continued military aid, despite the fact that it looms large in the total American foreign aid program. On the other hand, a redesigned bilateral aid program emphasizing assistance programs that deal directly with the pressing problems of the poor majority in the developing countries would attract support if the public understood its specific objectives and was persuaded of its greater potential effectiveness.

In 1974, a crucial item on the policy agenda will be trade. At present, decisions are being taken in the U.S. Congress on the shape of a trade bill, and the United States, together with other nations, has begun to negotiate a new set of tariff agreements under the General Agreement on Tariffs and Trade (GATT). Most Americans do understand that trade is of vital importance to the poor countries and will support lower tariffs on their exports. The key item, however, will be an effective program of federal adjustment assistance for retraining and relocating those American work-

---

[5]For a detailed discussion of these issues, see Robert E. Hunter (ed.), *The United States and the Developing World: Agenda for Action* (Washington, D.C.: Overseas Development Council, February 1973).

ers who are affected adversely by freer trade with the developing countries. Without such a program, most Americans will consider freer trade with the poor countries a much less attractive proposition.

The United States also faces decisions in a number of other areas, including the redesigning of the world monetary system, a new regime for the oceans, and decisions to be made before the United Nations convenes its major World Population Year conference in the fall of 1974. In each of these cases, policy makers must either design policies that will also meet the needs and expressed objectives of the developing countries, or return to the constricting course of narrow national interest. As these decisions are made in both the Executive and Legislative branches, it would be well for those engaged in this process to bear in mind the results of this survey.

The public's response to this survey shows that the American people are basically sympathetic to the problems of the developing countries and can be persuaded to support more enlightened policies that are in our long-term interest. However, it will also take an enlightened national leadership both to create such policies and to marshall the public support needed to see them through the legislative process.

the author

Paul A. Laudicina has been Associate Fellow at the Overseas Development Council since January 1971. He has travelled extensively in East Africa and in Latin America, where he conducted United Nations sponsored research in 1970. The author was formerly Executive Director and founder of the U.S. Coalition for Development and is a member of the U.S. Committee for UNICEF. He has studied at Maryknoll College and the University of Chicago.

Survey Questionnaire and Record of Responses of National Population Sample

Note: All open-ended questions are marked with an asterisk. In the case of open-ended questions, only those answers offered by 10 per cent or more of the respondents are included in this Annex.

---

1. This is a survey about world problems. I would like to ask you first if you think that tension in the world is greater than it was 10 years ago, about the same, or has world tension eased during the last 10 years?

    Greater..67%
    About the same..18
    Eased 13
    Not sure.. 2

2. And to look ahead 10 years from now, do you think world tensions will be greater than they are today, about the same, or will world tensions ease during the next 10 years?

    Greater..38%
    About the same..24
    Ease..27
    Not sure...12

3. How about the general living conditions of most of the people in the world? Would you say that living conditions in the world today are better than, about the same, or not as good as they were 10 years ago?

    Better..63%
    About the same..18
    Not as good...15
    Not sure.. 4

4. And would you say that living conditions in the world 10 years from now will be better than, about the same, or not as good as they are today?

    Better..49%
    About the same..22
    Not as good...17
    Not sure...11

5a. How much do you feel the United States government is doing at this time to fight domestic poverty? Is it doing more than it should, about the right amount, or less than it should?

    More than it should...13%
    About right..28
    Less than it should...54
    Not sure.. 5

5b. And do you think our government is doing more than it should, about the right amount, or less than it should to fight poverty in other parts of the world?

    More than it should...44%
    About right..31
    Less than it should...17
    Not sure.. 8

6a. Would you say the commitment of the United States government to help solve the problems of hunger and poverty in the world is very strong, fairly strong, or not strong at all?

Very strong..31%
Fairly strong 49
Not strong..15
Not sure.. 5

6b. And in your honest opinion — is your own personal commitment to help solve the problems of hunger and poverty in the world very strong, fairly strong, or not strong at all?

Very strong..20%
Fairly strong 43
Not strong..32
Not sure.. 5

6c. Concerning the problem of hunger and poverty, do you feel that people like yourself are doing all they can to solve it, as much as can be expected, less than expected, or almost nothing at all?

Doing all they can 14%
As much as can be expected..40
Less than expected..30
Nothing at all 13
Not sure 3

7. Here is a card showing some estimates in the U.S. budget for 1973. Looking at the amount of recommended budget for medical services, would you favor increasing the budget, keeping it the same, or cutting the budget for medical services?

	Increase	Keep Same	Cut	Not Sure
Medical services	51%	38%	6%	5%
Space research	13	39	44	4
National defense	10	46	38	6
Economic assistance to foreign countries	8	41	43	7
Farm price supports	32	38	18	13
Social Security	50	40	6	4
Military assistance to foreign countries	4	38	52	7
Food stamps	25	40	24	11
Education	68	26	3	3
Pollution control	65	26	5	5

8a.* In the context of world problems, what does the word *development* mean to you?

Improving living conditions, raising standard of living............. 13%
Helping people stand on their own feet,
    help themselves, self-improvement..................................... 12
Growth, building things up, getting stronger......................... 12

8b.* And what do the words *foreign aid* mean to you?

Helping, aiding other countries, people................................... 41%
Sending money to foreign countries.. 24
Sending food to foreign countries... 13
Handouts, give-aways, wasting money...................................... 13

9a.* If the United States decided to stop all of its economic foreign assistance programs, what do you think would happen to the countries we are now helping?

They would help themselves, would learn to
    rely on themselves, would get along................................... 23%

Communists (China, Russia) would take over;
they'd go Communist..20
Their growth would stop; they'd go backward
to where they were 16
They'd collapse, would go downhill fast, fall apart 13
They would get help from someone else,
would turn to others for help...11
They would starve; hunger 10

9b.* And if the United States decided to stop all of its economic foreign assistance programs, what effects do you think it would have on the United States over the long run?

Would be less popular, lose friends, allies;
would be hated, have more enemies; would
hurt relations with other countries....................................20%
We would have more money to spend at home,
more money to fight domestic problems............................17
Would lose trade, import prices would rise.............................10
Not sure, don't know 14

10. Here is a list of different countries in the world.

A. Which two or three countries on this list do you feel you know the most about?
B. And about which two or three countries on the list do you feel you know the least?
C. Which two or three countries on the list would you say have the highest standard of living?
D. And which two or three countries would you say have the lowest standard of living?
E. If you had your say about our foreign assistance, which two or three of the countries on this list would you first assist?
F. Why would you select these countries to assist?
G. And which two or three of the countries on the list would you least favor giving assistance?
H. Why would you least favor giving assistance to these countries?

	A. Know Most	B. Know Least	C. Highest Standard	D. Lowest Standard	E. Most Favor Assistance	G. Least Favor Assistance
Argentina	11%	9%	32%	2%	10%	5%
Bangladesh	9	30	1	33	24	2
Bolivia	2	19	3	3	4	1
Brazil	14	5	27	1	10	4
Chile	6	10	4	4	7	4
Mainland China	25	12	11	11	4	39
Egypt	16	6	7	4	4	12
India	24	3	2	38	29	3
Indonesia	5	9	1	7	7	2
Kenya	3	21	2	8	6	1
Nigeria	4	12	2	9	7	2
Pakistan	9	6	1	19	13	3
Peru	4	13	3	5	6	1
South Africa	15	7	16	11	10	8
South Korea	20	4	5	8	12	5
Soviet Union	52	4	39	2	1	57
Tanzania	0	52	1	5	3	2
None of the above	10	5	3	2	7	5
Don't know	8	10	27	23	23	23

F.* Why would you select these countries to assist?

They are the poorest, have the lowest standard
of living, need it most, have the most problems 24%
They need our help, just need it...13
They are hungry; need food 13
Are overpopulated; suffer problems of overpopulation 10

Have had recent problems, wars, inner turmoil 10
Have heard more about them on TV, radio, newspaper.......... 10
Don't know, not sure.. 12

H.*   Why would you favor these countries least for assistance?

They can take care of themselves, don't need us.................... 26%
They are Communist, do not want to support Communists.... 17
They are our enemies, oppose us, not our friends,
    hostile, would harm us, we are competitors,
    threat to security 14
Don't know, not sure... 12

11a.   Here is a list of various world problems that have been mentioned by
people like yourself. How serious do you consider each problem — very
serious, somewhat serious, or not serious at all? If you do not think it is
a problem, just say so.

(Responses to questions 11a, 11b, and 11c appear in table on p. 101.)

11b.   Now, if you were to set priorities, which two or three problems on the
list should receive top priority consideration, in your opinion?

11c.   Now, considering the problem of _____ ,
which countries does it affect more — rich countries or poor countries,
or does the problem affect everyone in the world just about the same?
(Asked for all problems considered either "very serious" or "somewhat
serious.")

12a.   And now if you were to estimate the number of people in the world
who are now living in underdeveloped countries, what would you say?

Less than ten percent... 5%
About one quarter 22
About one half... 28
About three quarters... 22
About ninety percent... 5
Not sure 19

12b.   How much would you say problems faced by poor people in the world
affect the people of the United States — a great deal, somewhat, or
hardly any at all?

Great deal 30%
Somewhat.. 36
Hardly any 25
Not sure 10

13.*   In what ways would you say the problems of other people in the world
affect us in the United States? (Asked of those who answered "great
deal" or "somewhat" in above question.)

Takes money out of the country, have to keep sending aid,
    keeps us from solving our own problems............................ 15%
Affects us economically 15
Does affect us because we help, we're expected to help;
    it's our responsibility to help 12
Costs us extra taxes.. 11
If affects our attitudes, what we think and what we do 11
Affects us militarily; we get involved 10
Not sure, don't know.. 9

14a.   Concerning the United States giving foreign assistance — would you say
you are strongly in favor, somewhat in favor, somewhat against, or
strongly against the United States giving assistance to underdeveloped
countries?

Strongly in favor... 16%
Somewhat in favor.. 52
Somewhat against 19

Responses to Questions 11a, 11b, and 11c

	A. Seriousness of Problem					B. Priority	C. Problem Affects			
	Very Serious	Somewhat Serious	Not Serious	Not a Problem	Not Sure	Top Priority	Rich Countries	Poor Countries	Everyone	Not Sure
Too much automation	16%	28%	27%	20%	9%	2%	54%	7%	32%	8%
Socialism	19	29	23	12	17	4	14	21	54	11
Corrupt government	54	30	8	3	5	23	13	14	70	3
Hunger and poverty	69	24	5	1	1	41	3	43	52	2
Too much technology	7	16	33	3	15	1	46	10	30	15
Trade barriers	9	31	26	13	22	1	18	19	51	12
Religious wars	33	29	18	10	10	5	6	21	61	12
Communism	54	25	11	4	6	20	5	23	67	5
Using up natural resources	59	23	6	4	7	18	24	4	69	3
Overpopulation	50	28	12	5	5	16	2	36	60	2
Lack of communication among people	50	31	11	4	5	14	7	10	80	3
Poor medical care	48	33	12	4	3	17	2	43	52	2
Hatred between racial and ethnic groups	55	32	8	2	3	17	10	7	79	4
Pollution	62	27	6	2	3	24	20	4	74	3
Illiteracy	37	37	14	5	7	9	2	52	43	3
Lack of adequate housing	38	40	14	4	5	7	3	47	48	3
Capitalism	17	26	22	19	16	2	30	11	50	9
Drug abuse	78	16	4	1	2	46	20	3	76	1
Corporate power	28	31	15	9	18	3	51	6	36	7
Territorial disputes	19	31	20	12	18	2	9	19	60	12

Strongly against 9
Not sure... 4

14b.* Why do you feel that way?

The wealthy should help the poor; people should help
each other, we should share, feed hungry people,
they need it... 27%
We should help our own first, take care of our own 17
It's our obligation, responsibility, Christian duty,
it is our moral duty.. 11

15a. Here are some statements concerning the total United States budget for
fighting hunger and poverty both domestically and internationally.
With which statement do you agree the most?

The total budget should be used for domestic poverty............ 13%
A small percentage of the budget should be used to fight
poverty in other parts of the world 55
The budget should be divided about fifty-fifty between the
poor of the U.S. and the poor in other parts of the world .. 18
The budget should be divided proportionally so that most
of it would go to help the poor in other parts of the
world 6
Not sure 8

15b. If you were told that 95 per cent of the poor people in the world lived
in other countries, and the United States had only 5 per cent of the
world's poor, would you reconsider your distribution of money?

Yes, would reconsider 26%
No, would not reconsider.. 59
Not sure.. 15

15c. Now, considering these statements once again, with which statement do
you agree the most? (Asked of those who answered "yes" to above
question.)

The total budget should be used for domestic poverty............ 4%
A small percentage of the budget should be used to fight
poverty in other parts of the world 9
The budget should be divided about fifty-fifty between the
poor of the U.S. and the poor in other parts of the world .. 35
The budget should be divided proportionally so that most
of it would go to help the poor in other parts of the
world 53
Not sure 5

16a. As you probably know, the United States is only one of many countries
that has economic foreign assistance programs. When you compare the
wealth of the United States to that of other wealthy countries, such as
Sweden or Canada, would you say our economic foreign assistance
budget is relatively greater than, about the same, or less than foreign
assistance programs of other wealthy countries?

Greater... 69%
Same... 11
Less... 2
Not sure... 18

16b. And, in your opinion, *should* our economic foreign assistance budget be
greater than, about the same, or less than other countries' in comparison with our wealth?

Greater... 20%
Same... 55
Less... 12
Not sure... 13

17a. Some people have said that there will always be wealthy people and there will always be poor people. Do you believe that poverty could be virtually eliminated in the United States within the next fifty years, or not?

> Poverty could be eliminated...38%
> Poverty could not be eliminated 56
> Not sure.. 6

17b. And do you think poverty could be virtually eliminated in the world within the next fifty years?

> Poverty could be eliminated...15%
> Poverty could not be eliminated 76
> Not sure.. 9

17c. Would you say that the gap between the rich and poor people in the United States has widened in the past ten years, is about the same, or that the gap between rich and poor people in the United States is narrower than ten years ago?

> Gap has widened...34%
> Gap about the same 31
> Gap is narrower..28
> Not sure.. 7

103

17d. And would you say the gap between rich countries and poor countries has widened in the past ten years, is about the same, or that the gap between countries is narrower than ten years ago?

> Gap has widened...31%
> Gap about the same 33
> Gap is narrower..19
> Not sure...17

18a. When the United States gives economic assistance to underdeveloped nations, would you say that it is mostly in the form of loans that are supposed to be repaid, or do you think it is mostly in the form of grants that do not have to be repaid?

> Loans...35%
> Grants..47
> Neither... 9
> Not sure..16

18b. And if you were to choose the kind of financial assistance we give to underdeveloped nations, do you think it should be mostly as loans, or mostly as grants that do not have to be repaid?

> Loans...68%
> Grants..17
> Neither... 5
> Not sure..11

18c. For loans that we have already given underdeveloped countries, do you feel that the loans are usually completely repaid, mostly repaid, only partially repaid, or not repaid at all?

> Completely repaid.. 4%
> Mostly repaid 5
> Partially repaid...51
> Not repaid at all 31
> Not sure..10

19a.* If you had to explain to someone why poor people are poor, what would you say?

> Lack of education, ignorance, illiteracy 43%
> Lazy, no ambition, no drive, don't get out
> and work, want to be poor, prefer welfare........................40

Lack of opportunity, never had a chance, can't get
decent jobs, don't have equal opportunity 25
They are born into it, the only life they know,
it's environmental, they inherit it 19

19b.* As you know, there are many countries in the world that are underdeveloped. How would you describe an underdeveloped country? What
are some of the main characteristics of an underdeveloped country?

Poor educational facilities, undereducated, illiterate 40%
Not enough technology, manufacturing, industry,
no exports for trade 24
Poor economy, low standard of living, poverty stricken 20
Can't feed their own people, hunger 19
Limited natural resources, poor land, no tools 12
Bad housing 12
Poor government, unstable governments that exploit 12
Do not use their resources to the fullest,
do not work up to their potential 11
Poor medical facilities, much illness, disease,
high mortality 10

19c.* What would you say are the most important reasons for a country like
ours to help an underdeveloped country?

For moral, humanitarian reasons; our responsibility.
We should, ought to. They need it. We should
help mankind 29%
To help them help themselves, to make them
self sufficient 18
We have so much, have disproportionate share
of wealth. Help balance wealthy nations and
poor nations 13
To have them as friends, allies; we may need
help someday 10

20. Here is a card with different statements concerning help given to
underdeveloped countries. Which statement comes closest to your own
view?

Underdeveloped countries can make it on their own
without help from the outside 6%
Underdeveloped countries need a little help from the outside
to get to the point when they can stand on their own 50
Underdeveloped countries will need a great deal of help for
a long time before they can become self-sufficient 30
No matter how much help underdeveloped countries are given,
they will never be able to make it without help from the
outside 9
Not sure 5

21a. This is a list of some of the things that can be done as foreign
assistance. Considering aid for medical care, would you say that it is a
very effective form of assistance, somewhat effective, or not effective at
all in helping underdeveloped countries? (Asked for each type of
assistance listed.)

(Responses to Questions 21a, 21b, and 21c appear in table on p. 105.)

21b. Now, which two or three of the methods of assistance listed here would
you favor the most as foreign assistance policy for the United States?

21c. And which two or three of the methods of assistance listed here do you
favor the least as foreign assistance policy for the United States?

22. Now here is a card with a scale on it from minus three to plus three. I
am going to read you some words and I want you to tell me how you
feel about the words. If you have strong positive feelings about the
word, you would say plus two or plus three. If you have strong negative

Responses to Questions 21a, 21b, and 21c

	Very Effective	Somewhat Effective	Not Effective	Not Sure	Favor Most	Favor Least
Send medical help, doctors and nurses	63%	31%	4%	3%	52%	1%
Encourage investment of U.S. corporations in these countries	22	43	21	14	8	21
Lower tariffs, open trade	22	44	14	20	5	11
Send machinery	40	43	12	5	8	8
Aid in birth control	50	28	13	9	26	9
Give financial grants	21	41	27	11	6	34
Send food, clothing	53	38	7	2	27	4
Train their students in our universities	55	31	9	6	29	7
Send technicians, engineers	49	37	8	6	16	4
Provide military training and equipment	11	33	45	10	1	49
Send teachers, books	59	33	5	4	27	3
Provide spiritual training, missionaries	38	37	20	6	13	18
Help underdeveloped countries sell their products in the United States	34	44	12	10	8	11
Provide low-interest loans	32	44	14	10	9	13
Send tractors, fertilizers, seed	53	35	7	5	19	6

feelings, you would say minus two or minus three. If you have mild feelings one way or the other, you would say plus one or minus one. If you have no feelings about the word, say *zero.* If you don't know the word, just say so. Now, for the word *cooperation,* what number on the scale would you select?

	Negative				Positive			Don't know word/
	-3	-2	-1	0	+1	+2	+3	Not sure
Cooperation	2%	3%	3%	7%	16%	31%	34%	5%
Foreign assistance	8	11	11	8	32	20	8	4
Development	2	1	3	9	26	30	23	5
Foreign aid	8	9	12	8	32	19	7	4
Capitalism	10	8	12	22	14	10	10	13
Social justice	4	3	4	14	18	17	27	13
Free trade	4	6	9	17	25	18	13	10
Population control	4	2	4	10	18	18	38	5
Isolationism	18	12	13	23	7	4	3	20
United Nations	6	4	7	14	23	19	21	6
Import taxes	4	6	11	20	24	16	9	11
Communism	42	11	14	12	5	4	7	5
Protectionism	5	4	9	22	15	10	11	22
Redistribution of wealth	12	8	9	21	16	10	12	13

106

23a. Here is a list showing different groups that help people in under-developed countries. For each group mentioned on the list, do you think the job it does in helping people in underdeveloped countries is very effective, only somewhat effective, or not effective at all?

	Very Effective	Somewhat Effective	Not Effective	Not Sure
Peace Corps	50%	38%	6%	6%
Religious groups	33	48	13	6
World Bank	11	30	16	43
YMCA/YWCA	18	39	18	25
United Nations	29	43	17	11
U.S. Corporations	15	45	19	21
CARE	50	37	5	8
Private foundations	17	46	15	22
Red Cross	51	33	10	6
UNICEF	38	34	7	21

23b. It has been suggested that the United States government should give more of its foreign assistance money to organizations like the ones on this list and give less money directly to the countries. Do you feel that the U.S. government should give money to organizations or should it give the money directly to the governments of the countries themselves?

Give money to organizations...57%
Give money to countries..22
Not sure...21

23c. If the U.S. government did decide to give more foreign assistance money to organizations like those on the list, which two or three organizations would you favor the most for receiving money?

Peace Corps..57%
Religious groups..29
World Bank 6
YMCA/YWCA.. 8
United Nations..13
U.S. Corporations 3
CARE 46
Private foundations.. 6
Red Cross...46
UNICEF..28
Other _____ 1
         (write in)
Not sure... 5

24a. Have you ever personally contributed money to an organization that works to help people in underdeveloped countries?

Have contributed 74%
Have not contributed 22
Not sure.. 4

24b. To which organizations have you contributed money? (Asked of those who answered "Have contributed" to above question.)

Peace Corps... 8%
Religious groups..39
World Bank.. 1
YMCA/YWCA..12
United Nations... 2
U.S. Corporations 1
CARE 33
Private foundations... 6
Red Cross...64
UNICEF..50
Other _____ 5
                        (write in)
Not sure... 1

25a. As you know, the United States puts import taxes, quotas, and other barriers on products coming in from various countries. Considering products coming in from wealthy countries such as West Germany and Japan, would you say you strongly approve, mildly approve, mildly disapprove, or strongly disapprove of import restrictions on goods coming in from wealthy countries?

Strongly approve..44%
Mildly approve..28
Mildly disapprove.. 9
Strongly disapprove 6
Not sure...12

25b. And considering the products coming in from underdeveloped countries, would you say you strongly approve, mildly approve, mildly disapprove, or strongly disapprove of import restrictions on goods coming in from underdeveloped countries?

Strongly approve..14%
Mildly approve..30
Mildly disapprove...21
Strongly disapprove 18
Not sure...16

26a. There has been a great deal of discussion on the idea of free trade between the United States and underdeveloped nations — that is, the lowering or elimination of restrictions on products coming from these countries. Here are some of the things that have been said by people who favor free trade. Which one of these statements is the most important reason to favor free trade as far as you are concerned?

More export jobs.. 9%
Helps underdeveloped countries...40
Lower prices 14
Stimulate competition 18
Not sure...18

26b. Now, here are some statements by those who oppose free trade. Which one statement is the most important reason to oppose free trade, as far as you are concerned?

Unfair competition 14%
Intensity of problem of trade balance....................................14
Put American laborers out of work 49
U.S. too dependent.. 5
Not sure...18

26c. Now that you have read some of the arguments about free trade with underdeveloped countries, would you say you basically favor the idea of free trade, or oppose it?

```
Favor ............................................................................41%
Oppose...........................................................................34
Not sure.........................................................................25
```

26d. If American workers who lost their jobs because of free trade did not suffer any personal financial loss and were retrained in jobs equal to or better than their old ones, would you basically favor the idea of free trade, or oppose it? (Asked of those who were "opposed" or "not sure" in above question.)

```
Favor ............................................................................44%
Oppose...........................................................................26
Not sure.........................................................................30
```

27a. Have you ever traveled outside of the United States?

```
Yes, have traveled ..........................................................52%
No, have not traveled ......................................................48
```

27b. If you added together all of the time you have spent traveling, how much time would you estimate you have spent outside the United States? (Asked of those who answered "yes" to above question.)

```
One month or less...........................................................48%
2-4 months.....................................................................13
5-7 months......................................................................5
8-11 months.....................................................................3
1 year or more ................................................................31
```

27c. Which parts of the world have you personally visited?

```
North America (Canada, Mexico).......................................71%
Western Europe................................................................26
Eastern Europe ...............................................................11
Asia................................................................................9
Middle East .....................................................................6
Far East ..........................................................................13
Central America ...............................................................5
South America .................................................................7
Africa..............................................................................5
Other _____.................................................14
      (write in)
```

27d. Would you say that your traveling was mostly for business reasons, for educational purposes, to work abroad, for military service, or for pleasure?

```
Business ..........................................................................3%
Educational......................................................................5
Work...............................................................................3
Military or other government service...................................29
Pleasure..........................................................................58
Not sure ..........................................................................1
```

28a. In which part of the United States did you spend most of your youth? The East, the South, the Midwest, or the West?

```
East................................................................................32%
South.............................................................................25
Midwest .........................................................................29
West...............................................................................12
Outside the U.S................................................................2
Not sure .........................................................................—
```

28b. In your youth, did you live mainly in a city, in the suburbs, in a small town, or on a farm?

City 32%
Suburb 15
Small town 28
Farm 24
Not sure 1

29. And would you say that in your youth your family was lower income, middle income, or upper income?

Lower income 39%
Middle income 56
Upper income 4
Not sure 1

30a. Now I would like to know how important you feel television has been as a source of information for you in learning about the various problems in the world. Is television very important, somewhat important, or not important at all? How about the newspapers? Have they been very important, somewhat important, or not important at all as a source of information to you?

(Responses to questions 30a, 30b, and 30d appear in table below.)

30b. And of these sources of information, which two or three would you say are the most reliable?

30c. *Why do you feel that these are the most reliable sources?

They are there, on the scene, on the spot;
    most coverage 15%
They are quick, up to date, inform me daily 13
I'm exposed more to it, it's more accessible.
    That's where I get all my news; it's all we have 12

30d. And which two or three of these sources would you say are the least reliable?

30e. * Why do you feel that these are the least reliable sources?

They are biased, onesided, prejudiced 17%
Based on opinions, their own views,
    exaggerations, other sources 17
They give false information, not factual,
    not truthful, not always well informed 12
Just don't read/listen to them,
    just don't rely on them 12

	A. Importance				B. Most Reliable	D. Least Reliable
	Very Im-portant	Somewhat Im-portant	Not Im-portant	Not Sure		
Television	64%	29%	6%	1%	64%	11%
Newspapers	62	31	7	—	52	16
Radio	42	41	16	1	27	7
School	40	34	22	4	13	6
Family	28	38	31	3	8	14
Friends	21	45	33	2	3	34
Church	23	36	38	3	12	16
Special meetings	12	29	53	6	4	22
Magazines	25	43	28	4	12	17
Books	30	40	27	3	10	9
Pamphlets and newsletters	16	40	39	5	4	30
Your work experience	25	32	38	5	8	14
Your personal experience	33	36	26	5	17	9

31a. And have you ever volunteered your spare time to an organization that was involved in helping people in underdeveloped countries?

Have volunteered 17%

Have not volunteered 81
Not sure 2

31b. If you were asked to give time to an organization that helped people in underdeveloped countries, would you be more willing to help an organization that was backed by our government or would you be more willing to help a private organization?

More willing to help government organization 34%
More willing to help private organization 34
No difference 19
Not sure 13

32a. If you were asked to volunteer your time or contribute money, would you prefer to help poor people in the United States or would you rather help poor people in underdeveloped countries?

United States 83%
Underdeveloped countries 6
No difference 8
Not sure 4

32b. Would you say that poor people in the United States basically have things better, about the same, or worse than poor people in other countries?

Better 68%
About the same 23
Worse 3
Not sure 6

33. Now I am going to read to you a list of statements that have been made by other people we have interviewed. For each statement, I want you to tell me if you agree strongly, agree somewhat, disagree somewhat, or disagree strongly with the statement?

(Responses to this question appear in table on p. 111.)

34a. As you know, many things have changed over the past ten years. Would you say your attitudes and opinions concerning the problems of the world are almost the same as those of the young people in your family, very much the same, fairly different, or completely different from those of the young people in your family?

Almost the same 23%
Very much the same 25
Fairly different 24
Completely different 16
Not sure 11

34b.* In what ways would you say that you are most different from the young people in your family in your feelings about the problems of the world?

We are about the same, don't really disagree 23%
Don't agree with their outlook on life, just different 12%
We differ on Vietnam, foreign policy; foreign aid 10%
No children or children too young 10%

35a. I'd like to ask in which countries your grandparents were born.

U.S. & North America 65%
Western European countries 27
Eastern European countries 10
Soviet Union 2
Arab countries .... **
China & Far East 1
Africa 1
South America .... **
Central America .... **

Responses to Question 33

	Agree Strongly	Agree Somewhat	Disagree Somewhat	Disagree Strongly	Not Sure
The United States already has a large budget deficit and cannot afford to help underdeveloped nations	23%	29%	29%	11%	8%
Our government should do more to encourage businessmen to invest in underdeveloped countries	19	36	20	12	14
The U.S. is doing more than its fair share in helping underdeveloped countries	50	29	12	3	6
If we do not help other countries, the Communists will take them over	37	29	17	9	8
Too much foreign aid is wasted in our own bureaucracy and never finds its way abroad	46	27	9	4	14
The United States exploits poor countries just to get what it needs	7	17	26	38	13
Too much of our foreign assistance money is kept by the leaders of poor countries and does not get to the people	46	30	6	2	16

(continued)

111

Responses to Question 33 (Continued)

	Agree Strongly	Agree Somewhat	Disagree Somewhat	Disagree Strongly	Not Sure
Foreign aid should come from voluntary contributions rather than taxes	30	27	20	11	12
We help some countries because it is morally right to do so	31	45	11	5	8
It is more important to help the poor people in this country first before doing anything in foreign assistance	63	20	9	3	3
We help some countries because poverty breeds violence	28	40	13	7	11
The United States should pay back the money corporations lose when they are nationalized by other countries	4	9	22	42	23
Countries that receive foreign assistance should have the right to determine how to spend the money	12	29	26	22	12
It is really in the best interest of the United States to help poor countries	31	46	11	4	8
Without trade with other countries, the U.S. would suffer considerable economic hardships	33	33	15	7	12
The U.S. should help only those underdeveloped countries that will support a democracy	27	26	21	12	14

Other_____ 5
    (specify)
Not sure.. 2
    **(Less than one per cent)

35b. And when you think back about your family heritage, with which countries of the world do you identify?

U.S. & North America.......................................36%
Western European countries.........................42
Eastern European countries 10
Soviet Union.. 1
Arab countries .... **
China & Far East.. 1
Africa... 4
South America.. **
Central America... **
Other _____ 7
    (specify)
Not sure... 6
    **(Less than one per cent)

36a. Would you say that you have ever personally experienced hunger and poverty?

Yes, have experienced......................................27%
No, have not experienced................................72
Not sure... 1

36b. Have you ever lived in a situation where your neighbors suffered from hunger and poverty?

Yes, have..40%
No, have not 58
Not sure... 3

36c. Would you say you know a great deal about hunger and poverty, some but not much, or hardly anything?

Great deal 23%
Some, but not much 51
Hardly anything...25
Not sure... 1

37a. Are you registered to vote at this time?

Yes, registered...81%
No, not registered ,...18
Not sure... 1

37b. Are you registered as a Democrat, Republican, or Independent? (Asked of those registered to vote.)

Democrat...52%
Republican..26
Independent..16
Other 3
Not sure... 4

38a. Now here is a card with a scale describing the political views of different types of people. Where would you place yourself on the scale?

38b. And for the young members of your family, where would you say they are on the scale politically?

		a. Self	b. Young in family
(Radical Left)	1	2%	2%
	2	3	3
(Liberal)	3	11	14
	4	8	8
(Moderate)	5	41	28
	6	9	6
(Conservative)	7	15	9
	8	2	1
(Ultra-conservative)	9	1	1
Not sure		8	29

114

Survey Sampling Technique[1]

Philosophy Utilized in Sample Design

The national sample cross section design has been done with the purpose of maximizing the useful stratification which may be employed to produce a sample with greatest accuracy for a fixed sample size. We have tried not to introduce excessive refinements, but have followed the strategem of stratifying where possible and introducing random elements (which insure that we achieve a truly random sample that is projectible) at the lowest possible level.[2]

A careful examination of the distribution of the youth population (those eighteen to twenty-five years of age) and the adult population (eighteen years and older) has indicated that the distribution of these two segments does differ by fractions of a per cent, but there is no place where the difference is such that a separate sample for the two elements would be justified. Therefore, we have used the adult population as the basic frame for both samples. If we were dealing with a sample size of 50,000 or more, the theoretical imperfection of the youth sample using an adult sample framework might be great enough to cause us to change our basic strategy. But, in practical terms, with a sample size of 1,200 the standard error of estimate is of sufficient size to mask in an overwhelming fashion any imperfections which this frame represents for the youth sample.

115

Stratification of the National Sample

The stratification employed in the construction of this national sample follows the rough outlines of procedures for the development of national samples by the leading market research firms in the United States. These considerations deal with not only the potentially theoretically desirable stratifications; but also with the factors which have been found to really matter in a large number of sociological, business, and political inquiries implemented through the methodology of survey research.

The basic stratification employed is that of region within the United States. Repeatedly, differences in view have been exhibited among the East, Midwest, South, and West. We have followed the definition of these regions employed by the Census. Within a region the next most important differences in opinion have been those associated with the most urban and lesser urban parts. Thus the data on population has been stratified on the basis of cities, suburbs, other urban, and rural. This stratification is even more refined in the context that within a region cities have been ordered from largest to smallest, associated suburban parts also have been ordered from largest to smallest, and the other urban population strata have been geographically spread as have been the rural population strata. This strategy of organization is similar to that adopted by the Wooldridge Committee in its study of the National Institute of Health Program.[3] This type of stratification scheme assures that every region, and every size of city, suburb, town, and rural area will be included within one percentage point of its actual distribution within the total population.

Once the adult population (for purposes of the general population sample, eighteen years and older) of the United States has been arrayed in this manner, a tape is prepared with each major unit (cities, suburbs, other urban by state, and rural by state) represented by proper subtotals. A random selection tape is constructed using the following device. In order to bring intra-cluster correlation effects to a minimum, and still keep costs of interviewing at a reasonable level, we selected a cluster size of six interviews,

---

[1]Excerpted, with minor revisions, from the study on American attitudes toward international development conducted by Peter D. Hart Research Associates, Inc., Washington, D.C. for the Overseas Development Council (1972).

[2]W. G. Cochran, *Sampling Techniques*, 2nd ed. (New York: John Wiley & Sons, Inc., 1973).

[3]*Biomedical Science and its Administration,* A Study of the National Institute of Health, Report to the President, February 1965.

thereby requiring 200 sample points for a sample of 1,200 respondents. We then divided the total adult population of the United States eighteen years and older by 200. This number, the sampling interval, is then multiplied by a random number, to give a random starting point.

The above procedure defines the sample in terms of gross units. The sample is further refined by the use of tract and block information in those areas for which such information exists, in that the tract material can be accumulated to the actual point within the selected area, and hence unique blocks selected. Outside of tracted areas, similar techniques can be used to define explicit towns, or minor civil divisions, and random area's selection is made within these small units.

The results of utilizing these procedures can be seen in the following table which gives the characteristics of the U.S. adult population and corresponding sample points.

	U.S. Adult Population		Sample Points	
Total	133,567,845	100%	200	100%
East	33,014,905	25	49	25
Midwest	36,732,026	28	56	28
South	40,959,216	30	61	30
West	22,861,698	17	34	17
Cities	43,599,090	33	66	33
Suburbs	35,204,430	26	52	26
Other Urban	20,722,528	16	32	16
Rural	34,041,797	25	50	25

The selection of households within the selected areas is done utilizing random starting points, and the selection of individuals within the households for interview is also done utilizing random selection procedures. From the random starting point, the interviewer is directed in a systematic manner, so that this freedom of choice in household selection is minimal.

Two call backs were made for selected households, and complete records were kept of the results of each attempt at contact. When the designated respondents were not at home, appointments were made, and call backs at the appointed time were employed. The call backs were spread over different times of the day to insure that there was a maximum chance of contact being made.

Two random selection procedures for respondents within a household were utilized, one for the adult sample and one for the youth sample. The basic difference in the procedures is that the eligibility of youth in the non-college youth sample was restricted by age (eighteen to twenty-five years) and by the fact that they are not attending college.

The College Youth Sample

The college youth sample was constructed by a random selection of students from college campuses. We obtained up-to-date enrollment figures from the National Center for Educational Statistics of the U.S. Department of Health, Education, and Welfare. These figures were used to build a frame stratified by region, type of college (public or private), and by size of college within region within type. From this frame, forty colleges were selected and ten students were interviewed at each college.

Procedures for Final Analysis

All college youth were obtained from the college youth sample, and no college youth were obtained in the eighteen to twenty-five year old youth national cross section. These two segments were melded in appropriate proportions to obtain the material for the aggregate youth sample.

Similarly, the youth sample was appropriately weighted into the adult national cross section.

After weighting had been applied, the youth sample and adult sample were completely projectible to their respective populations.

Both the adult sample and the youth sample are of nominal size (1,200), and the weighting procedures applied did not change this nominal effective size very much. The standard error is very near the value of 1.7 per cent, which could be expected from a sample of 1,200 with this degree of clustering.

General Population Sample[a]

	Sample Size	Per Cent
Total	1203	100%
Sex		
Male	593	50
Female	605	50
Age		
18–25	242	20
26–35	278	23
36–50	334	28
Over 50	333	28
Education		
College Graduates	154	13
Some College	137	11
High School Graduates	440	37
Non-High School Graduates	360	30
Occupation		
Professional/Executive	267	23
White Collar	172	17
Blue Collar	438	24
Income		
Under $7,000	359	30
$7,000–$15,000	430	45
Over $15,000	245	20
Race		
White	1044	87
Black	129	11
Other	23	2
Region		
North East	291	24
North Central	341	28
South	361	30
West	209	18
Size of Place		
City	377	33
Suburban	291	26
Town	177	16
Rural	275	25
Religion		
Protestant	727	61
Catholic	298	25
Jewish	27	2
Other	69	6
None	73	6

[a]The sample was weighted by age. All of the numbers shown here are adjusted by the weighting process. See the section on "weighting" for greater detail.

Youth Sample Overview

	Sample Size	Per Cent
Total	**1222**	**100%**
Sex		
Male	623	51
Female	594	49
Age		
18	203	17
19	178	15
20	147	12
21	173	14
22	107	9
23	94	8
24	137	11
25	170	14
Race		
White	1057	87
Black	134	11
Other	22	2
Marital Status		
Married	444	37
Single	742	61
Other	28	2
Region		
North East	292	24
North Central	336	28
South	348	28
West	246	20
Size of Place		
City	273	34
Suburban	217	27
Town	123	15
Rural	196	24
Family Income		
Under $7,000	337	28
$7,000–$15,000	458	38
Over $15,000	322	26
Religion		
Protestant	559	46
Catholic	323	27
Jewish	46	4
Other	102	8
None	184	15
College Experience	703	58
Non College	519	42
In College Now[a]	413	34
Freshman	114	28
Sophomore	100	24
Junior	84	20
Senior	72	17
Graduate Student	43	10
Major[a]		
Humanities/Social Science	126	31
Science/Math	50	12
Business	55	14
Engineering	23	5

	Sample Size	Per Cent
Education	60	14
Other	94	23
Size of School[a]		
Under 6,500	123	30
6,500–20,000	137	33
Over 20,000	153	37

[a]Percentages based on students only.

Weighting

A complete study of approximately 1,200 people between the ages of eighteen and twenty-five was conducted separately from the general population study. A separate sampling of individuals over twenty-six years of age was conducted simultaneously. A total of 999 people over age twenty-six were interviewed. To meld these two studies together in proper proportion so that we would have an accurate general population sample of 1,200 respondents, it was determined that we would weight the youth sample by a factor of two tenths. Thus, overall, the general population sample is a statistically reliable cross-section of all adult Americans over the age of eighteen. For the youth study, the sample did not require weighting.

119

Sampling Error and Statistical Significance Tables[1]

Sampling Error

Although many people find it hard to believe that a sample of 1,200 can represent the population of the United States, this is nonetheless statistically true. However, in reading the data, it should be kept in mind that the results are subject to sampling error, i.e., the difference between the results obtained from the sample and those which would be obtained by surveying the entire population. The size of a possible sampling error varies to some extent with the size of the sample and with the percentage giving a particular answer. The following table sets forth the range of error in samples of different sizes and at different percentages of response. Thus, for example, if the response for a sample size of 1,200 is 30 per cent, in 95 cases out of 100, the response in the population will be between 27 per cent and 33 per cent.

Recommended Allowance for Sampling Error (Plus or Minus)
At 95 Per Cent Confidence Level

Per Cent of Response	Sample Size				
	1,200	900	500	250	100
10% (90%)	2%	2%	3%	5%	7%
20% (80%)	3	3	4	6	10
30% (70%)	3	4	5	7	11
40% (60%)	3	4	5	7	12
50%	3	4	5	8	12

Significance of Difference

When is a difference between two results significant? As in the case of sampling error, the answer depends on the size of the samples involved and percentage giving a particular answer. The following table has two charts, one showing the significance of difference between different-sized samples when the per cent giving an answer is near 50 per cent and the other showing the significance of difference when the per cent giving an answer is near 20 per cent or 80 per cent. Thus, for example, if one group of size 900 had a response of 56 per cent "yes" for a question and an independent group of size 250 had a response of 43 per cent "yes" for the same question, in 95 cases out of 100, the difference in the "yes" response rate for these two groups would be 13 per cent (56 per cent minus 43 per cent), plus or minus 8 per cent, or between 5 per cent and 21 per cent.

---

[1]Adapted from the study on American attitudes toward international development conducted by Peter D. Hart Research Associates, Inc., Washington, D.C. for the Overseas Development Council (1972).

Recommended Allowance for Significance of Difference Between Two Percentages at 95 Per Cent Confidence Level

1st Sample Size/ 2nd Sample Size	% of Response Near 50%				
	1,200	900	500	250	100
1,200	5%	5%	6%	8%	12%
900	5	6	7	8	12
500	6	7	7	9	13
250	8	8	9	11	14
100	12	12	13	14	17

1st Sample Size/ 2nd Sample Size	% of Response Near 20% or 80%				
	1,200	900	500	250	100
1,200	4%	4%	5%	7%	10%
900	4	4	5	7	10
500	5	5	6	7	10
250	7	7	7	8	11
100	10	10	10	11	13

The Sympathy and Information Indices

Sympathy Index

The sympathy index is a measurement of a respondent's basic attitudinal orientation to assisting the process of development in the poor countries. This index was developed from a selection of the nine survey questions thought to be the best indicators of public opinion on both governmental and personal commitment to solving global poverty problems.

Respondents could score a minimum of zero and a maximum of four on each of the nine questions. The maximum score, indicating support for development issues examined, was thirty-six points; the lowest possible score of zero indicated basic opposition to development concerns. Obviously, no single response by itself offers an accurate indication of development sympathy or opposition. Yet, if a respondent scored twenty or higher on the index, he was designated as being in basic sympathy with the problems of poor countries and peoples and desirous of assisting those countries in solving their problems. (Such a respondent would support a vigorous U.S. international effort on trade and assistance policy.) The nine questions comprising the index are listed below.

1. How much do you feel the United States government is doing at this time to fight domestic poverty? Is it doing more than it should (0 points), about the right amount (2 points), or less than it should (4 points)?[1]

2. Do you think our government is doing more than it should (0 points), about the right amount (2 points), or less than it should (4 points) to fight poverty in other parts of the world?

3. In your honest opinion, is your own personal commitment to help solve the problems of hunger and poverty in the world very strong (4 points), fairly strong (2 points), or not strong at all (0 points)?

4. If you were to set priorities, which two or three problems on the list should receive top priority consideration in your opinion? Answer: Hunger and poverty (4 points).

5. Concerning the United States giving foreign assistance—would you say you were strongly in favor (4 points), somewhat in favor (3 points), somewhat against (1 point), or strongly against (0 points) the United States giving assistance to underdeveloped countries?

6. Considering the products coming in from underdeveloped countries, would you say you strongly approve (4 points), mildly approve (3 points), mildly disapprove (1 point), or strongly disapprove (0 points) of import restrictions on goods coming in from underdeveloped countries?

7. Do you agree strongly (0 points), agree slightly (1 point), disagree somewhat (3 points), or disagree strongly (4 points) with the following statement: the United States already has a large budget deficit and cannot afford to help underdeveloped countries?

8. Do you agree strongly (0 points), agree slightly (1 point), disagree somewhat (3 points), or disagree strongly (4 points), with the following statement: the United States is doing more than its fair share in helping underdeveloped countries?

9. Do you agree strongly (4 points), agree slightly (3 points), disagree somewhat (1 point), or disagree strongly (0 points), with the following statement: we help some countries because it is morally right to do so?

---

[1]Sympathy index question number one, which dealt with domestic poverty, might, at first view, seem out of place in this attitudinal measurement. Yet, the addition of this question was judged to be important, given the conceptual inseparability of domestic and global poverty issues in the minds of the project organizers.

The sympathy index is most useful in showing different levels of response of various socio-economic groups. This index only indicates relative support on a broad range of issues comprising the needs of the underdeveloped countries today. Absolute support for specific aid proposals is discussed in Chapter III.

An individual was considered basically unsympathetic on international development issues if he scored fourteen or lower on the sympathy index. Someone who scored between fifteen and nineteen was considered "uncommitted"—i.e., ambivalent to the problems of the poor countries.

An analysis of answers to the individual questions comprising the index reveals that those social groups—persons of a certain age, party, or education—with higher percentages of pro-development answers than others on one question will similarly score comparatively high on other questions. For example, 63 per cent of the college graduates sampled were in favor of the United States giving foreign aid (Question 5), while only 50 per cent of those who have not completed high school answered similarly. In contrast, the question about the United States doing its fair share for development (Question 8) showed lower support for development than demonstrated by any other question on the index. Just 21 per cent of the college graduates felt that the United States was doing less than its fair share—but only 6 per cent of those who have not completed high school felt likewise. Therefore, answers to both questions show higher support among college graduates for improving the lot of the poor countries than among any other educational category. This pattern is similar for six of the nine individual questions, as well as for the whole index itself.

Thus the sympathy index conveniently summarizes the results of the individual questions. The index was composed independently of the survey results; had questions 3, 4, and 9 not been included in the index, correlations shown in Chapter VI would be far stronger.

Information Index

The second index developed for the analysis of the data of this survey was called the information index. While this survey was not conducted for the primary purpose of determining how much Americans knew about the objective facts and figures of development, a number of questions in the survey did provide us with some measure of how well informed the public is on development issues. We already know from previous surveys cited in this monograph that very few Americans have over the years consistently scored high on information questions regarding the foreign assistance program. Alfred Hero states, "Less than one adult out of ten has known or guessed within a billion dollars of the correct figure of the overall aid budget. Similarly, small minorities have known or guessed, that foreign aid has constituted less than 5 per cent of the national budget, or less than one per cent of the GNP. . . . "[2] We did not, therefore, repeat objective questions of that nature. We did, however, examine the level of public awareness on a few of the issues which one would expect a "well-informed" public to score high. The five questions comprising this index are shown below.

1. Which two or three countries on the list have the highest standard of living?

Argentina	Mainland China	Nigeria	Soviet Union
Bangladesh	Egypt	Pakistan	Tanzania
Bolivia	India	Peru	None of the Above
Brazil	Indonesia	South Africa	Don't Know
Chile	Kenya	South Korea	

Answer: Any 2 of the following countries: Soviet Union, Argentina, South Africa, Brazil, Chile (2 points)

2. Which two or three countries would you say have the lowest standard of living?

[2]Alfred O. Hero, Jr., "American Public Reactions to Development Assistance" (Study prepared for the Brookings Institution Steering Committee on a possible new organization to develop U.S. public support for aid, Washington, D.C., 1968), p. 54.

Answer: Any two of the following countries: Tanzania, Nigeria, India, Bangladesh, Indonesia, Pakistan (2 points)

3. If you were to estimate the number of people in the world who are now living in underdeveloped countries, what would you say: Less than 10 percent, about one quarter, about one half, about three quarters, about ninety per cent, not sure?
Answer: About three quarters (3 points)

4. As you probably know, the United States is only one of many countries that has economic foreign assistance programs. When you compare the wealth of the United States to that of other wealthy countries, such as Sweden or Canada, would you say our economic foreign assistance budget is relatively greater than, about the same, or less than foreign assistance programs of other wealthy countries?
Answer: Less than (1 point)

5. For loans that we have already given underdeveloped countries, do you feel that the loans are usually completely repaid, mostly repaid, only partially repaid, or not repaid at all?
Answer: Completely repaid (1 point)

An individual who scored nine on the information index received a perfect score. Any respondent who scored five or above was judged to be informed on development issues. Similarly, anyone who scored zero was judged to be uninformed on development issues. Since each of the information index questions does not carry the same importance as a gauge of development information awareness, different values or weights were assigned to the scoring of the five questions. Question three, regarding the population size of the developing world relative to that of the industrialized world, was judged to be the most important question for an informed respondent to answer correctly and was therefore assigned a weight of three points. Questions one and two, regarding the relative wealth and poverty of a number of countries, were considered next in importance on the information index and were assigned weights of two points each. Questions four and five were judged non-essential increments of information for a respondent to have and hence were assigned weights of one point each.

Only those questions considered to be clearly objective and to measure relatively important facts for an informed respondent to know were selected for use in the information index. Since the information index was not intended to be a precise mechanism for determining the knowledge of respondents, we chose to analyze only the responses at each extreme of the index— i.e., those respondents very informed, and those very uninformed scoring zero.

Bibliography

Public Opinion on Development Issues (Surveys)

Hero, Alfred O., Jr. "Foreign Aid and the American Public," *Public Policy* 14 (1965), pp. 71-116.

Lindholm, Stig. *The Image of the Developing Countries: An Inquiry into Swedish Public Opinion.* Uppsala, Sweden: The Dag Hammarskjold Foundation, 1971.

Padrun, Ruth. "Attitudes and Motivations of Manual Workers in Industry Concerning Development Issues" (Report of an International Pilot Study prepared for Action for Development of the U.N. Food and Agricultural Organization). Paris: International Institute of Research and Training in Education and Development, August 1972.

Rauta, I. *Aid and Overseas Development: A Survey of Public Attitudes, Opinions and Knowledge.* London: Her Majesty's Stationery Office, 1971.

"Survey on Opinions and Attitudes in the Netherlands Concerning Development Cooperation." The Hague: Netherland's National Committee for Development Strategy 1970-1980 (July/August 1971).

Youth on Development: Survey of Opinions of Canadian Youth on International Aid and Development. Ottawa, Canada: Canadian Council for International Co-operation, 1971.

Public Opinion and Foreign Policy

Allison, Graham T. "Cool It: The Foreign Policy of Young America," *Foreign Policy* 1 (Winter 1970-71), pp. 144-60.

Bauer, Raymond A.; Pool, Ithiel de Lola; and Dexter, Lewis. *American Business and Public Policy: The Politics of Foreign Trade.* New York: Atherton Press, 1963.

Bonilla, Frank. "When is Petition 'Pressure'?" *Public Opinion Quarterly* 20, no. 1 (Spring 1956), pp. 39-48.

Campbell, Angus; Converse, Philip E.; Miller, Warren E.; and Stokes, Donald E. *The American Voter.* New York: John Wiley & Sons, 1960.

Caspary, William R. "The 'Mood Theory': A Study of Public Opinion and Foreign Policy," *American Political Science Review* 64, no. 2 (June 1970), pp. 536-47.

Cohen, Bernard C. *The Influence of Non-Governmental Groups on Foreign Policy-Making.* Boston: World Peace Foundation, 1959.

———. *The Press and Foreign Policy.* Princeton: Princeton University Press, 1963.

———. *The Public's Impact on Foreign Policy.* Boston: Little, Brown and Company, 1973.

Ellenport, Samuel. "American Foreign Policy and Mass Democracy," *American Scholar* 36 (Autumn 1967), pp. 589-93.

Hennessy, Bernard C. *Public Opinion.* Belmont, California: Wadsworth, 1965.

Hero, Alfred O., Jr., *American Religious Groups View Foreign Policy: Trends in Rank-and-File Opinion, 1937-1969.* Durham, N.C.: Duke University Press, 1973.

———. *The Southerner and World Affairs.* Baton Rouge: Louisiana State University Press, 1965.

Johnson, James A. "The New Generation of Isolationists," *Foreign Affairs* 49, no. 1 (October 1970), pp. 136-46.

Kahn, Harlan. "Political Efficacy and Foreign Policy Attitudes," *Social Problems* 17 (Fall 1969), pp. 271-9.

Kelman, S. J. "Youth and Foreign Policy," *Foreign Affairs* 48 (April 1970), pp. 414-26.

Key, V. O., Jr. *Public Opinion and American Democracy.* New York: Knopf, 1971.

Kolko, Gabriel. *The Roots of American Foreign Policy: An Analysis of Power and Purpose.* Boston: Beacon Press, 1969.

125

Kristol, Irving. "American Intellectuals and Foreign Policy," *Foreign Affairs* 45, no. 4 (July 1967), pp. 594-609.

Lacy, Virginia P. "Political Knowledge of College Activist Groups: SDS, YAF, and YD," *Journal of Politics* 33 (August 1971), pp. 840-5.

Lane, Robert E., and Sears, David O. *Public Opinion.* Englewood Cliffs, N.J.: Prentice Hall, 1964.

Laulicht, Jerome. "Canadian Foreign Policy Attitudes: Some Major Conclusions," *International Social Science Journal* 17, no. 3 (1965), pp. 472-86.

May, Ernest R. *American Imperialism: A Speculative Essay.* New York: Atheneum, 1968.

Miller, Warren E., and Stokes, Donald E. "Constituency Influence in Congress," *American Political Science Review* 57, no. 1 (March 1963), pp. 45-56.

Modigliani, Andre. "Hawks, Doves, Isolationism and Political District," *American Political Science Review* 66, no. 3 (September 1972), pp. 960-78.

Modigliani, Andre, and Gamson, William A. "Knowledge and Foreign Policy Opinions," *Public Opinion Quarterly* 30 (Summer 1966), pp. 87-99.

O'Leary, Michael Kent. *The Politics of American Foreign Aid.* New York: Atherton Press, 1967.

Robinson, James A. *Congress and Foreign Policy-Making.* Homewood, Ill.: Dorsey Press, 1967.

Robinson, John P. *Public Information About World Affairs.* Ann Arbor: University of Michigan, Institute for Social Research, 1967.

Rogers, William C., and Uhlig, Barney. "Small Town and Rural Midwest Foreign Policy Opinion Makers," *International Studies Quarterly* 13, no. 3 (September 1969), pp. 306-25.

Rogers, William C.; Stuhler, Barbara; and Koenig, Donald. "A Comparison of Informed and General Public Opinion on U.S. Foreign Policy," *Public Opinion Quarterly* 31 (Summer 1967), pp. 242-52.

Rosenau, James N., ed. *Domestic Sources of Foreign Policy.* New York: Free Press, 1967.

_____. *National Leadership and Foreign Policy.* Princeton: Princeton University Press, 1963.

Smith, Paul A. "Opinions, Publics, and World Affairs in the U.S.," *Western Political Quarterly* 14, no. 3 (September 1961), pp. 698-714.

Yarmolimsky, Adam. "Confessions of a Non-User," *Public Opinion Quarterly* 27, no. 4 (Winter 1963), pp. 543-8.